PUFFIN BOOKS

Anne Frank and the Children of the Holocaust

Carol Ann Lee's interest in Anne Frank began when she was six years old, after reading a book about the young diarist. Her first book, *Roses from the Earth: The Biography of Anne Frank*, was published in 1999 and has been translated into fifteen languages. Her other books include *The Hidden Life of Otto Frank* (a biography of Anne's father) and two books for children: *Anne Frank's Story* and *A Friend Called Anne*. For six years, Carol Ann Lee lived in Amsterdam, but she has recently moved back to the UK and now lives in York, with her son, River.

Books by Carol Ann Lee

For children

Anne Frank's Story

A Friend Called Anne
(*with Jacqueline van Maarsen*)

For adults

Roses from the Earth:
The Biography of Anne Frank

The Hidden Life of Otto Frank

Anne Frank

and the Children

of the Holocaust

CAROL ANN LEE

Foreword by Buddy Elias, cousin of Anne Frank

PUFFIN

PUFFIN BOOKS

Published by the Penguin Group
Penguin Books Ltd, 80 Strand, London WC2R 0RL, England
Penguin Group (USA) Inc., 375 Hudson Street, New York, New York 10014, USA
Penguin Group (Canada), 90 Eglinton Avenue East, Suite 700, Toronto, Ontario, Canada M4P 2Y3
(a division of Pearson Penguin Canada Inc.)
Penguin Ireland, 25 St Stephen's Green, Dublin 2, Ireland (a division of Penguin Books Ltd)
Penguin Group (Australia), 250 Camberwell Road, Camberwell, Victoria 3124, Australia
(a division of Pearson Australia Group Pty Ltd)
Penguin Books India Pvt Ltd, 11 Community Centre, Panchsheel Park, New Delhi – 110 017, India
Penguin Group (NZ), cnr Airborne and Rosedale Roads, Albany, Auckland 1310, New Zealand
(a division of Pearson New Zealand Ltd)
Penguin Books (South Africa) (Pty) Ltd, 24 Sturdee Avenue, Rosebank, Johannesburg 2196, South Africa

Penguin Books Ltd, Registered Offices: 80 Strand, London WC2R 0RL, England

penguin.com

First published 2006
1

Text copyright © Carol Ann Lee, 2006
Maps copyright © Tony Fleetwood, 2006
All rights reserved

The moral right of the author and illustrator has been asserted

Set in Sabon and Rotis Sans Serif
Typeset by Palimpsest Book Production Limited, Polmont, Stirlingshire
Made and printed in England by Clays Ltd, St Ives plc

British Library Cataloguing in Publication Data
A CIP catalogue record for this book is available from the British Library

ISBN-13: 978-0-141-31963-6
ISBN-10: 0-141-31963-1

For Linda

Contents

	Map	viii–ix
	Foreword by Buddy Elias	xi
	Introduction	xiii
1.	'As We Are Jewish . . .'	1
2.	'We Emigrated to Holland . . .'	17
3.	'When We Were Still in Normal Life . . .'	31
4.	'Good Times Rapidly Fled . . .'	50
5.	'When the Sufferings of Us Jews Really Began . . .'	61
6.	'It's an Odd Idea for Someone Like Me to Keep a Diary . . .'	78
7.	'We Have to Whisper and Tread Lightly . . .'	92
8.	'I Am Afraid of Prison Cells and Concentration Camps . . .'	120
9.	'Who Has Inflicted This Upon Us?'	139
10.	'I Want to Go On Living Even After My Death . . .'	157
	The Anne Frank Trust UK	175
	Further Reading	177
	Acknowledgements	179
	Photo Credits	181
	Sources	183

Foreword

This book is important – not only for young people, but for all ages. No doubt you will have heard about the Holocaust in school, seen films about it in the cinema or on TV, and read many stories and novels in which the Nazis try to conquer Europe. And you have probably read the world-famous diary of Anne Frank, the young girl who spent two years hiding from the Nazis with her family in the Secret Annexe. Yet despite all this, you still have many unanswered questions and want to know more about the terrible events of the Holocaust. When did it all start? What caused it and why? What happened to Anne and her family after they were betrayed and arrested? Who was responsible for the murder of one and a half million children? Why were Jews branded as 'vermin' by the Nazis? And why were the Sinti and Roma people, Jehovah's Witnesses and other minorities also victims of Nazi persecution?

Here you will find the answers to these questions and more. You will discover who the *Einsatzgruppen* were, and what happened in Babi Yar and Auschwitz. You will learn about Hitler's cruel 'Euthanasia' project during which thousands of disabled children and adults were killed by so-called doctors and nurses. You will read about the heroes who, at great risk to themselves, saved the lives of many. And you will not only find out more about Anne Frank, but also read eyewitness reports of the Holocaust from other children, some who survived and some who did not.

Carol Ann Lee's book will make you realize what discrimination can do. I would urge you not to allow it to happen in your school or neighbourhood, but to keep your eyes open and take a firm stand against racism or anti-Semitism whenever or wherever you are confronted with it.

This book might change your life and help you to make this a better world.

Bernd 'Buddy' Elias
Cousin of Anne Frank

Introduction

In September 1939, when the Second World War began, more than one and a half million Jewish children were living in countries occupied, or soon to be occupied, by Hitler's armies. By 1945, when the war ended, over a million of those children – including Anne Frank – were no longer alive.

They were not killed by bombing raids or in the line of duty; they were deliberately murdered by the leaders and followers of a political party who believed they had no right to live, simply because they were Jewish. Other children whose ethnic origin or religion, or whose parents' political choice meant that they had no place in a Nazi-led society, were also targeted.

Because the Nazis were in power for so long (from 1933 to 1945), thousands of children never had a normal childhood. Something as simple as going to a local swimming pool with friends or kicking a football around in a park during the summer evenings was strictly forbidden. They were banned from ordinary activities like going to the cinema. After war broke out in 1939, these same children faced an even more terrible future: often torn from their families, they were pushed into ghettos* or into slave labour camps, where starvation and disease raged. Thousands more were killed by firing squads.

In the summer of 1942, mass deportations began, with trains rolling out of every occupied country, taking Jews to the concentration camps in eastern Europe. Children were sent, either with their families or alone, to the camps, where hardly any of the very young survived; they were not able to work hard and therefore the Nazis had no use for them. Most children under the age of fifteen were killed. Girls were less likely to survive than boys because they were seen as the weaker sex and could give birth. The Nazis wanted to ensure that Jewish life was destroyed, not created.

Despite all this, children often turned out to be braver and more capable than many adults. Being so young, they were able to adapt more quickly to certain situations. In the ghettos, for example, children smuggled in food and sold anything they could find to raise money for their families. They also refused to give in to despair: they sang songs, made their own games and toys, and studied schoolbooks, even though all these activities were forbidden. Like Anne Frank, many children kept diaries, using whatever paper was available to them. They wrote in office ledgers, on scraps of newspaper, and even – in the case of a young brother and sister in the Lodz ghetto – in the margins of an old French novel.

* *Ghettos*: Sealed-off areas of towns where the Jews were forced to live in extreme poverty.

The diary of Anne Frank is the best known, and she has become a symbol of all the children who died during the Holocaust. In total, six million Jews were killed by the Nazis. Such a huge number is hard to imagine. But, in the same way that we can learn more about Anne Frank's world by understanding the Holocaust, by looking in detail at her short life we begin to understand that 'six million' means six million individuals who once had hopes and dreams for the future, just like us. In this way, we realize that the Holocaust isn't about impossible numbers; it's about people.

1

'As We Are Jewish . . .'

Anne Frank was born in the German city of Frankfurt-am-Main
on 12 June 1929. Her grandfather was a country boy who
came to Frankfurt to make his fortune. He opened his own
banking business in the city and married a young woman whose
ancestors had lived in Frankfurt for over four hundred years.
Anne's father, Otto, was born on 12 May 1889 (the same year
as Adolf Hitler) and he enjoyed a happy, privileged childhood.
He and his two older brothers, Robert and Herbert, and their
younger sister, Leni, were brought up in a large house in
Frankfurt's Westend district. Their home was filled with
antiques and enormous family portraits in gilt frames. At the
back was a large garden; the front overlooked an elegant
square.

Anne later wrote that her father had had 'a real little rich
boy's upbringing, parties every week, balls, festivities, beautiful
girls, waltzing, dinners, a large home, etc'.[1] A photograph of a
family gathering in Germany's Black Forest in 1900 shows Otto
Frank (then ten years old) in a crisp white sailor suit – the
trendiest outfit for boys at that time – while Leni, Robert and
Herbert are also fashionably dressed. They all attended good

schools, spoke several languages, learned how to ride, and played musical instruments. Anne loved to hear her father talk about his childhood when she was in hiding; to her it seemed like a distant fairy tale.

When Otto Frank was eighteen, he began studying economics at Heidelberg University. There he met Nathan Straus, whose family owned Macy's department store in New York. Nathan and Otto quickly became good friends, and when Nathan went back to America, he invited Otto to join him there and to work in Macy's, which was then the world's biggest department store. Otto eagerly accepted, juggling his time at Macy's with another job in a New York bank. Then one day Otto received a telegram telling him that his father had died, and he returned to Germany. He found a new job with an engineering company in Dusseldorf and was still working there when war broke out in 1914.

Although the Franks were Jewish, they did not show much interest in their religion. Otto rarely attended synagogue and he didn't read or speak Hebrew, the ancient Jewish language. The district where the Franks lived was popular with many Jewish families and it had a synagogue at its centre, but Otto was brought up to take more pride in his German roots than in his religion. Not long after the war began, he and his brothers joined the German army, and his mother and sister worked in hospitals, taking care of wounded German soldiers.

By now Otto was in his twenties, a natural leader who was friendly and fair with everyone he met. He was made a junior officer and then a lieutenant, and he proved himself a brave soldier on the Somme and at Cambrai, two of the worst battles in history. He was certain that his country would win the war, but in 1918 Germany surrendered and Otto returned to Frankfurt.

The Franks' banking business had lost a great deal of money during the war. Otto tried to improve the situation by opening a branch of the bank in Amsterdam, where business was better than it was in Germany. Unfortunately, this wasn't a success, and once more he went back to Frankfurt. Otto was now thirty-six years old. He had been engaged when he was nineteen, but it hadn't worked out, and now he was eager to marry and have children.

He met Edith Hollander, then twenty-five, and found that, despite her shyness, she was kind and intelligent and shared his interest in art, literature and family life. She was also a modern young woman who loved fine clothes, dancing, music, and holidays with her large circle of relatives and friends. She was one of four children; her sister, Betti, had died of appendicitis at the age of sixteen, but Edith was close to her two older brothers, Julius and Walter, who had also served in the German army. Like Otto's, her childhood in the German city of Aachen (close to the Dutch border) had been happy and secure, and her father was a successful businessman who had made a lot of money dealing in scrap metal. Edith was more religious than Otto; her family attended synagogue regularly and kept a kosher household, observing the Jewish dietary laws.

Otto and Edith married on 12 May 1925 in the synagogue in Aachen, where the Hollanders were lifelong members of the congregation. After a honeymoon in Italy the couple returned to Frankfurt, where they lived with Otto's mother for two years.

Both Otto and Edith looked forward to being parents and were overjoyed when their first child, Margot Betti, was born on 16 February 1926. A peaceful baby who slept through the night almost from birth, with a shock of dark hair and big, wondering eyes, Margot was her mother and father's 'little angel'. She grew into a quiet, well-behaved child, eager to please everyone and with a sunny outlook on life. She was eighteen months old when her parents decided they needed a place of their own. They found a large apartment to rent on Marbachweg, in an unfashionable part of Frankfurt. The apartment was on two floors of a huge house, with a balcony overlooking the houses behind theirs. Margot had her own bedroom, next door to her parents' room, and there was also a room for their housekeeper, Kathi, a cheerful young woman whom Margot adored.

As the months passed and Margot became a toddler, she made friends with a girl named Hilde, who lived in one of the other apartments, and with Gertrud, a slightly older girl who lived in the house next door. Hilde and Gertrud were Catholics, and Mr and Mrs Frank encouraged Margot to take an interest in her friends' religion, which she did, playing 'church' with Hilde in her apartment and attending Hilde's Communion party.

There were other children living on the ground floor of the house too, but neither Margot nor Hilde nor Gertrud played with them: their father was the landlord and was a keen supporter of the Nazi Party. His children never tried to make friends with Margot, Hilde or Gertrud. They had probably been forbidden to play with Margot, for by this time a gulf was opening up between Jews and non-Jews in Germany that would one day sweep through Europe on a tidal wave of hatred.

The Franks' landlord was just one of several thousand supporters of the growing Nazi Party. The Nazis promised a bright future for Germany, and they singled out the Jews as the root of the country's problems, which had begun with the end of the Great War in 1918. The countries which had won the war, including Britain, France and the United States, put together the Versailles Treaty in 1919. This was basically a list of rules which Germany had to obey as punishment for starting the war. Under the treaty, Germany had to give up some of her land and pay for the damage – a colossal sum – caused by the war. The German army and navy also had to be cut back, and the entire political structure of Germany had to be altered according to the new rules. These points deeply angered many Germans, who felt humiliated by the treaty.

All this had a disastrous effect on the German economy, causing inflation and unemployment to soar. Nevertheless, a new Germany arose, called the Weimar Republic, more democratic than before and based on an elected parliament (housed in the Reichstag). Among those committed to rebuilding Germany were many Jews. But there was someone else, too, who wanted to make Germany great again, someone who saw the opportunity to grasp power and create a nation unlike any other in Europe.

His name was Adolf Hitler.

Born in a small Austrian town in 1889, Hitler had fought in the German army in the war and had won the Iron Cross for bravery. He had always dreamed of becoming an artist but, when the war ended with Germany's defeat, he decided to go into politics instead. When the National Socialist German Workers' Party (NSDAP or Nazi Party) was created in 1920, Hitler immediately became a member; and he saw himself as future leader of the Party. He hoped to lead the Nazis to victory in the German parliament and he set out a programme for them to follow.

Among Hitler's policies for the Party was that only those people who were of German blood and therefore 'members of the Nation' could class themselves as German citizens. Under these absurd rules, Jewish people were not entitled to German citizenship. He demanded that Jews who had entered Germany after 1914 should be expelled from the country, and when he addressed a crowd in a Munich beer hall in August 1920, his theme was: 'Why We Are Against the Jews'. He talked of a 'thorough solution' to ridding Germany of its Jews.

For a while it seemed that Hitler would fail in his political ambitions. He was jailed after trying to seize power from the existing government. Most of his time in prison was spent writing his deeply anti-Semitic* book, *Mein Kampf* (*My Struggle*). But when he was released from prison, he quickly became leader (*Führer*) of the Nazi Party.

---

* *Anti-Semitic*: Jew-hating.

In 1929, the New York stock market crashed, causing a worldwide depression and making the economic crisis in Germany even worse. Hitler knew that people were looking for someone to blame and were seeking a way out of their problems. He offered them both, holding the German government and the Jews responsible for the country's misfortunes. He told voters that if they supported him, Germany would become the most powerful nation on earth. He said that he would ignore the terms of the Versailles Treaty and that the German people were not responsible for the high levels of unemployment and widespread poverty in the country. Hitler pointed his finger at the Jews, calling them dishonest, money-grabbing and dangerous. He branded them 'race polluters' and spoke of the 'pure' blood of non-Jewish Germans. According to Hitler, as members of the 'Aryan race', the Germans were the most advanced people on earth.

These ideas appealed to many Germans, who listened to Hitler spellbound. They wanted to regain their pride in themselves and their country. They had grown up with the idea that Jews were different: for many Germans, the Jews were associated with the Communist Party,* and the clothes and the religious beliefs of Orthodox Jews seemed sinister to them. Jealousy was also an issue: despite everything, Jewish people had worked hard to rise to the top of several professions and had built strong communities. They had an

* Communist Party: Political party whose members believe that everyone should contribute to society according to their abilities and receive according to their needs.

identity that many non-Jewish Germans felt they themselves lacked. Jews were the focus of Hitler's rage, although he also spoke out against black people, Roma and Sinti,* the mentally and physically handicapped, and homosexuals. To an enthusiastic Germany, Hitler declared that none of these groups could ever be part of the Aryan master race.

It was into this terrifying world that Anne Frank was born in 1929.

It was 7.30 in the morning, on 12 June 1929, when Annelies Marie Frank was born in Frankfurt's city hospital. Her birth had been long and difficult, and the nurses were so tired they accidentally wrote in the hospital register that the 3.75-kilogram baby was 'a male child'! Within a few hours of her birth, Anne had had her first photograph taken by her proud father and was given a necklace with on one side a Hebrew inscription, and on the other her birth date and the words 'Lucky Charm, Frankfurt'. Mrs Frank kept baby record books for both her daughters, and in the one for Anne she wrote: 'Mother and Margot visit the baby sister on June 14. Margot is completely delighted. Home on June 24. At night for six weeks she cries a lot. Julius and Walter [Anne's uncles from Aachen] arrive by car on July 6. Anne is suffering from the heat wave.'[2]

The baby's first smile, when she was just a month old, was for her father. Anne soon became a real daddy's girl, while Margot favoured her mother more. Mr Frank was a good father and, unusually for a time when men didn't generally play as

* *Roma* and *Sinti*: Also known as Gypsies.

active a role in their children's early life as they do now, he played with his daughters, bathed them, fed them, changed their nappies and told them stories before they went to sleep at night. Mrs Frank took care of her children during the day, but when Mr Frank came home from work, he liked to spend as much time with them as possible.

In August 1929, the family travelled to Aachen for a holiday with Mrs Frank's family, and little Anne cried all the way. In Aachen she settled down, and Mrs Frank wrote in the baby book that Anne was happy if someone, especially her Uncle Julius, came into her room in the mornings. Mrs Frank added, 'Anne does so many silly things. We return home on September 3. Anne sleeps all the way.'[3] These baby books tell us how different Anne and Margot were as children. Margot was always very quiet, well behaved and neat (Kathi called her 'the little Princess'), while Anne slept badly, cried a lot and was often quite naughty. This pattern continued as the two of them grew older. Mr and Mrs Frank always held Margot up as an example to Anne, who found this very frustrating and annoying. When they were very young, Margot and Anne were both popular girls and they loved fun and games, although Anne liked to get into mischief. When Anne was a toddler, Kathi found her one morning sitting on the balcony in the rain, in the middle of a puddle. She was giggling, and even when Kathi picked her up and scolded her, she didn't cry but asked if Kathi would tell her a story – while she, Anne, went back to her puddle!

Anne liked to have her own way, and she said things that she really shouldn't have. But she was such a lively, affectionate and friendly girl that no one could be cross with her for long.

Especially not her father, who was always the one who managed to get her to go to sleep at night by telling her the stories his mother had told him when he was young, about two sisters, Good Paula and Bad Paula. Anne loved these tales, and later she wrote one of her own, when she was in hiding.[4]

Despite their different characters, Margot and Anne played together often, and with Hilde and Gertrud too. Gertrud liked to babysit Anne, feed her and change her nappies. The girls played in Hilde's backyard, where there was a sandpit and a swing, but Anne and Margot were also frequent visitors at their grandmother's (Omi) house in the Westend of the city. Omi could be very firm and she had the air of a queen when she walked, but she was so kind that the girls loved her deeply and liked to cuddle up with her in bed when they stayed at her house. Omi was a real storyteller and wrote poetry too. Every week she would tell Margot and Anne about a group of mice that had adventures. Anne was always happy to listen to these stories. She was quickly growing into an observant, talkative little girl who liked to make people laugh and to be the centre of attention. Omi called her 'little woman' and said she had an old head on young shoulders.

Margot and Anne's bright, chatty aunt Leni (Mr Frank's sister) also lived in Omi's house with her husband and two young sons, Stephan and Buddy. Both boys loved to play tricks and pranks. When Anne was older, she and Buddy found that they shared a sense of humour and loved dressing up, but when Anne was still very small, Buddy and his brother Stephan liked to push Anne around the neighbourhood in her pram. One day out almost ended in disaster. Buddy remembers: 'My brother and I took Anne in her pram outside. We went racing around and around the street but we couldn't get the kerb right and the pram tipped up. Anne flew out of the pram! We told no one, of course, and Anne was OK.'[5]

Anne and Margot also looked forward to visits from their other grandmother (Oma) in Aachen and their uncles, Julius and Walter. Oma Hollander was very calm and quiet, and she took great interest in everything Margot and Anne said and did. She was angelic, like Margot; and Mr and Mrs Frank sometimes asked her not to be too soft with the children, especially with Anne, who was very strong-willed. Julius and Walter had no children of their own and they enjoyed spoiling the girls. Anne and Margot loved their uncles and, because their father didn't own a car, they were always excited when Uncle Julius or Uncle Walter offered to take them out in the car.

These early years in Frankfurt, so happy and carefree for Anne and Margot, were coming to an end. Their housekeeper, Kathi, who would soon be leaving them to get married and set up a home of her own, appeared one day looking troubled. When Mr Frank asked her what was wrong, she told him that she had spoken to the washerwoman, who said she had been unable to sleep the night before because of fighting in the streets caused by the Brownshirts. Kathi asked Mr Frank who the Brownshirts were. Mr Frank, fully aware that the Brownshirts were anti-Semitic Nazi thugs who attacked Jews at any opportunity, tried to make a joke out of it so that his children wouldn't become alarmed. But Mrs Frank said in a serious, quiet voice, 'We'll find out soon enough who they are, Kathi.'

*　　*　　*

The proper name of the Brownshirts was the SA.* They were Hitler's bodyguards, but their duties included attacking Jews and political opponents. The brown uniforms they wore led to their being known as 'Brownshirts' by everyone in the country. With the SA roaming the streets, Jews were no longer safe; there were assaults on Jews in cafés, theatres, shops and synagogues. Bystanders either watched curiously or walked away. Few dared to try to stop the violence.

As more people joined the Nazi Party, enormous parades and rallies were held, which in turn drew voters, just as Hitler had hoped. Often held in the evening and by torchlight, thousands of Nazis in their distinctive uniforms marched together, holding the red flag of the Nazi Party with its black swastika (an ancient religious symbol) in a white circle. They pledged to support Hitler, chanting '*Heil Hitler*' and thrusting out their right arms in the Nazi salute to their leader.

The parades and rallies were the most spectacular political events Germany had ever seen. Among those watching was Otto Treumann, a Jewish boy of fourteen: 'The media were completely in thrall to the Nazi Party. It took hold of you, whether you liked it or not. It was so nationalistic . . . feeling "German" and identifying with the Fatherland were extremely appealing, now that the country was scrambling to its feet after the defeat of 1918. Scary? Absolutely! Especially when you knew that you

* *SA*: Sturm Abteilung; branch of the Nazi Party organized as a military force.

were Jewish and that all the problems were being blamed on you.'⁶

Hitler knew that such displays would make an impression on young Germans whose loyalty was important to his future in politics. He formed the Hitler Jugend (Hitler Youth) for children between the ages of fourteen and eighteen, who were then expected to join the Nazi Party when they turned eighteen.

In September 1930, the Nazis won 107 seats in the Reichstag, making them the second largest political party in the country. When the new Nazi members of parliament arrived at the Reichstag that month, crowds of Hitler Youth stood outside to cheer them in. Holding the Nazi flag high and with their hands raised in the Hitler salute, thousands of boys and girls joined the older Party members in chanting, 'Germany awake! Death to Jews!'

The Frank family were forced to leave their home on Marbachweg in 1931, when their landlord told them that he no longer wanted Jews living in his property. Mr and Mrs Frank had already thought about moving anyway, since in their part of the city groups of Brownshirts often marched by, singing vicious songs about Jews. The Franks found a new home on Ganghoferstrasse, in a quieter, prettier part of Frankfurt, with fields nearby. Most of their neighbours were doctors and lawyers, and there were some Jewish families among the Christian ones. Nazi soldiers didn't march about on the streets of this suburb, and the house itself was nicer, with a garden and a sandpit in the yard. Margot and Anne made new friends quickly, and they saw their old friends too.

When summer came, Mrs Frank filled an old bathtub with water so that Anne and Margot could play in it on hot days. Anne was not allowed out of the garden alone, and her favourite spot was the sandpit, where she could play all day if Margot was out with older friends. In the winter, when it snowed, the fields nearby were perfect for tobogganing, and Anne loved being pulled around on a sledge by Margot or having snowballing competitions. They still played with their cousins, Stephan and Buddy, and they looked forward to holidays in Aachen with their mother's family, who often visited them in Frankfurt as well.

In the spring of 1932, Margot started school. It was quite close to home, and no one cared that she was one of the few Jewish girls in her class. She was well liked by everyone, and she proved herself to be a clever girl who worked really hard at her lessons. But she was never the swot Anne later teased her of being; she liked to be with her friends and play games or go cycling. She was still a quiet, polite girl and always would be. Anne was learning to talk very well, and sometimes she said things that embarrassed people. She was only a toddler when she and Oma got on a busy tram and no one gave them a seat, prompting Anne to pipe up: 'Won't anyone stand up for this old lady?' Whatever popped into Anne's head quickly popped out of her mouth.

While their father was working, Anne and Margot's mother would often take them into the town centre of Frankfurt. There were many shops and lots of pleasant little cafés, where Mrs Frank sometimes arranged to meet her friends. Anne and

Margot were happy to let her chat while they ate the delicious cakes on offer. Both girls were always as well dressed as their mother, who liked to buy clothes for her children as much as for herself. One photograph taken of them about this time shows Margot wearing a very smart outfit of shiny shoes, long socks, a skirt, smart jacket and a hat, and Anne in a fluffy white coat. They would usually visit one of the big department stores in town, before going home in time to greet Mr Frank when he returned from work.

After their evening meal and bath, Mr Frank read to his daughters or made up stories for them, just as he always had done. Both girls loved their father to spend time with them, and they gave him a special name: Pim. Mr Frank was as keen a photographer as always, and he took scores of pictures of Margot and Anne playing, reading or simply sitting together. They were exceptionally pretty little girls, with large, long-lashed eyes and the same thick, dark-brown hair as their mother.

Although their home life was happy, Nazism had gained a firm grip on the city of Frankfurt. Mr Frank tried to joke about the Nazis to his wife and children, but other friends and relatives remember that he was seriously worried about the future. Violence against Jews was growing more and more common, and the streets of Frankfurt were full of foul graffiti about Jews. Some Jewish-owned shops had their windows defaced with slogans in white paint, and the Nazi flag hung from many houses, shops and offices. The swastika was everywhere: on stamps and posters, even on cups and saucers. Every day, groups of Nazis would march through the streets, looking to cause trouble for the Jewish citizens of the city.

On 30 January 1933, Mr and Mrs Frank were visiting friends and listening to the radio when it was announced that Hitler had been appointed Chancellor of Germany. Their host said cheerfully, 'Well, let's see what the man [Hitler] can do!' Mr Frank later recalled, 'I could not reply, and my wife sat as if turned to stone.'[7]

The Nazi Party had gained enough votes in the elections to make them the party with the majority in the Reichstag. Germany was now under Nazi rule.

2

'We Emigrated to Holland . . .'

By 1933 it wasn't only the Nazis who were giving Mr Frank cause for concern: the banking business was failing and his income was far less than before. Anne's Omi (her father's mother) asked if they would prefer to give up their apartment and live with her, which would save them quite a bit, so at the end of March 1933, they moved in with Omi. Her house must have seemed huge to them after their apartment, and the girls had an even bigger garden to play in than before, although they were further away from their friends and from Margot's school. She began attending a new school nearby, but it was very different from her old one. This time, because she was Jewish, Margot had to sit apart from her 'Aryan' classmates, with the other Jewish children. Her parents were deeply unhappy about this and so was Margot; she liked to get along with everyone and had never suffered discrimination until then.

The segregation of Jewish and non-Jewish children at Margot's school led to Mr and Mrs Frank's decision to leave Germany. The year before, they had discussed emigrating. Mr Frank recalled, 'As early as 1932, groups of Brownshirts came marching by singing, "When Jewish blood splatters off the knife". This made it more than clear to everyone. I immediately discussed it with my wife: "How can we leave here?" but then there is also the question, "How will you be able to support yourself if you go away and give up more or less everything?"'[8]

Other family members had recently left Germany to begin new lives elsewhere. Anne and Margot's cousins, Buddy and Stephan, had moved with their parents to Switzerland, where their father was manager of Opekta, a company selling pectin* and producing other kinds of food. Otto Frank's brother Herbert had emigrated to Paris, and his other brother, Robert, was living with his wife in London, where they had opened an antiques business.

Mr Frank considered living with one of the other family members abroad, but he also needed a job of his own. His brother-in-law in Switzerland suggested that he open up a branch of Opekta in Amsterdam. Mr Frank liked the idea: it would get them all out of Germany to a place where he already had friends and which he knew quite well. He decided that this was the best answer to their problems, and in June 1933, he travelled by train from Frankfurt to Amsterdam.

Anne and Margot stayed behind with their mother in Omi's house until their belongings could be sent on to Aachen. They would live with Oma Hollander, Uncle Walter and Uncle Julius until their father found them a home in Amsterdam. When they left Frankfurt, Omi closed up the house where she had

---

* *Pectin*: A gelling ingredient used in jam-making.

lived for thirty years and took a train to Switzerland, where she moved in with her daughter's family.

After that, there were no members of the Frank family living in Frankfurt any more; Hitler was beginning to achieve his aim of making life in Germany so impossible for Jews that they had no option but to leave.

With the setting up of the Hitler Youth, Hitler had begun to turn his attention to Germany's youths and children. He banned all youth groups except those approved by the Nazi Party and made clear his ambitions:

A youth will grow up before which the world will tremble. I want a brutal, domineering, fearless, cruel youth. Youth must be all that. It must bear pain. There must be nothing weak and gentle about it . . . That is how I will create the New Order.[9]

Boys between the ages of six and fourteen were pressed into joining the Jungvolk (Young People), while those aged fourteen to eighteen were guided towards the Hitler Youth. There were two groups for girls: the Jungmadel (Young Girls), for girls between the ages of ten and fourteen, and the Bund Deutsche Mädel (League of German Girls) for those aged fourteen to eighteen. Thousands of boys and girls willingly joined, attracted by the sporting and camping activities promised by the Nazi Party. Their leaders told them that they were superior to everyone else and that they were needed to fight a battle of 'good versus evil' against Jews. Girls were not led to expect a career;

they were taught that motherhood should be their greatest aim – providing new blood for the Nazi state – and they were given lessons in housekeeping and childcare.

At the same time, Hitler stepped up his campaign against the Jews. One month after gaining power, the Nazi Minister of Propaganda, Joseph Goebbels, announced a nationwide boycott of Jewish-owned shops, Jewish doctors and Jewish lawyers. News of this reached Britain and America; in New York, some people protested against the planned boycott by asking everyone not to buy German goods. Their actions made little impression on the Nazis.

At ten o'clock on the morning of 1 April 1933, in villages, towns and cities throughout Germany, groups of Brownshirts headed towards shops, surgeries and law practices owned by Jews. They painted abusive graffiti on doors and smashed windows with heavy truncheons. Armed with revolvers, they stood outside the places they had attacked, warning people not to enter.

A young Jewish boy named Gerard Durlacher (later a famous writer) watched the boycott of his grandmother's shop. He could see the revolvers hanging from the belts of the brown-uniformed Stormtroopers as they stood squarely on either side of the doorway. The men were motionless but the air around them was charged with menace. Alongside them were huge placards that Gerard could not read, but which he understood were telling people that this shop was a Jewish shop and people were not to buy from it. Youths gathered around, shouting the slogans on the placard, while the adults nodded their approval and shouted that it was true, Jews were spoiling Germany and would prove to be the country's downfall. Gerard could only stand and stare as a group of youths painted white Stars of David on the windows of his grandmother's shop.

This boycott shocked many people, even those who had voted for Hitler. Most did not join in, as the Nazis had hoped, but walked quietly away. A few deliberately entered Jewish shops to show their disapproval and to let Jewish people know that not all Germans were admirers of Hitler. The Brownshirts grabbed these people on their way out and put a stamp on their faces that read: 'We, traitors, bought at Jewish shops.'

On 7 April, the Nazis brought in a law banning Jews, black people and other ethnic minorities from working at state schools. Hundreds of teachers were dismissed and replaced by Nazis. Hans Massaquoi, who was seven years old when Hitler became Chancellor, found that the new teachers were cruel to him, not because he was Jewish but because he was black. Many of them were openly unpleasant to him and made offensive remarks about black people to hurt him. Once, when Hans was about ten years old, a teacher took him outside the classroom and threatened, 'When we've settled the score with the Jews, you'll be next.'

All Jewish children attending schools with non-Jews were now made to sit apart from their classmates. They were humiliated and ridiculed by the teachers, who gave reading lessons from the new, Nazi-regulation textbooks. One teaching manual showed a boy drawing a 'Jewish' face on a blackboard above a caption informing pupils that all Jewish noses were bent, and looked like the number 6. Another booklet with the title *Victory of Arms, Victory of Children* had a photograph of a German family next to a Roma family and informed the reader, 'These are children of your own blood, and these belong to an alien race.'[10]

New lessons were introduced: Race, Genetics and Nation. Jewish children were brought to the front of the room and used as 'life objects'. In the small town where she lived, Clara Wachter Feldman was singled out by a new teacher who was a member of the Nazi Party. On his first day, the teacher looked at Clara and said, 'I understand we have a Jew pig in our classroom.' He walked across to Clara and began hitting her on the hand with a stick, telling the other pupils, 'Now we'll see how much pain a Jew pig can endure.'

At break-times children were encouraged to play the latest board game, 'Jews Out!'. Jewish children lived in an increasingly isolated world, ignored by their old friends and bullied by their classmates.

The April boycott was the first of a long line of anti-Jewish laws passed in 1933. Jewish civil servants were fired and Jewish companies were taken over by Nazis. New war memorials left off the names of Jewish soldiers who had died for their country. Towns and villages without a Jewish population displayed banners at their entrance proudly telling visitors that the place was 'Jew-free'. Jews were forced out of public life, banned from their jobs and from all leisure activities. Anyone who tried to resist was either imprisoned or executed.

On 1 May 1933, some 20,000 books by Jews, homosexuals and other forbidden writers were burned in front of the Berlin Opera House. From an open car, parked nearby, Joseph Goebbels watched the flames from the bonfire leaping high into the night sky, surrounded by cheering Nazis. He was glad to see the books being torn apart and thrown into the fire, for he believed them to be nothing but 'intellectual filth'.

Two months later, on 14 July, the Nazis brought in a law to prevent 'genetically unfit offspring' being born. The new ruling targeted mentally and physically handicapped people, epileptics, the blind and the deaf. They were taken to hospital and forcibly sterilized so that they could never have children. The Nazis believed that anyone who was handicapped was a drain on the state, and that money spent caring for them was wasted. At least 400,000 people were sterilized under this new law.

Among them was sixteen-year-old Franziska Schwarz. Franziska was born deaf; her parents were hard of hearing, but her brother and several other relatives had normal hearing. Franziska and her mother were ordered to report to a hospital for sterilization. The family appealed against the decision, and Franziska's mother was told that she didn't have to have the operation, but her daughter did. Franziska screamed during the entire journey to hospital. She was locked into a room with two other deaf girls and the three of them sobbed all night. During that night, a nurse arrived to give them tranquillizers. Franziska fought the nurse, but in the end she had to give in and have the injection. When she woke up, she found she had been put in a ward and, from the pain in her stomach, she knew that the operation had taken place. She began to cry bitterly. A nurse came over to give her a glass of water and she, too, was crying. 'I'm sorry,' said the nurse, 'there's nothing I could do to help you.' She glanced up at a portrait of Hitler that dominated the hospital ward and then looked down at Franziska. She tapped her finger against her forehead to show that she thought Hitler was mad; she did not dare say the words out loud.

Some 63,000 Jews left Germany in 1933, many finding refuge in lands they had never seen before, such as Venezuela, Bolivia, Japan and South Africa. Those Jews who stayed in Germany did so hoping desperately that things would improve. Many were too old, too poor or too sick to leave, and most people found it difficult to get away under any circumstances. They had to leave behind their way of life, their language, their culture, their relatives and their friends. Not all countries welcomed Jews and, as the number of refugees grew, escape routes began to close down when Britain, America, Holland and France – among several others – set limits on how many refugees they were willing to take in.

* * *

Margot and Anne didn't attend school in Aachen. Anne was still too young, and there was little point in finding a school for Margot when they hoped to be living in Amsterdam by the end of the year. Mrs Frank wrote to the girls' friend Gertrud, to let her know that they were happy in Aachen but were looking forward to living together as a family again. Mr Frank had taken lodgings in Amsterdam and had opened a branch of Opekta in the city centre. He spent his free time trying to find a suitable apartment for his family. Mrs Frank joined him at the weekends, leaving Anne and Margot safely in the care of Oma Hollander and uncles Julius and Walter.

They found an apartment at last at 37 Merwedeplein, in south Amsterdam's River Quarter, a busy area, popular with refugees from Nazi Germany. The suburb was still being built, and the square in front of the Franks' new home was a flat, green space with trees that were little more than young shoots, leaving the children of the neighbourhood with a small field on which to play games. The apartments were identical and were made of brown brick with large, white-framed windows and orange roofs. The Franks' apartment was on the third floor, with the sitting-room window overlooking the square, and with a gravel balcony at the back which Anne called 'the terrace' and which was big enough to take a couple of sunloungers. There were several shops in the area, lots of little cafés and bakeries set up by families fleeing Germany, and a real sense of community.

At the end of 1933 Margot arrived by car with her uncles Julius and Walter. Anne stayed in Aachen with Oma Hollander until February 1934, to give her parents a chance to organize everything and to allow Margot to get used to her new school. Four-year-old Anne arrived on Margot's birthday and later wrote in her diary that she was placed on the table as a surprise present for her older sister.

The family soon settled into their new home. Mr Frank's business was doing well. He had taken on a young woman in her twenties, Miep Santrouschitz, to act as his secretary, and she became a personal friend of the whole Frank family. Although Miep was born in Austria, she had lived in Amsterdam since she was eleven years old and considered herself to be Dutch. She hated the Nazi Party, as did Victor Kugler, who worked for Mr Frank as manager. He was Austrian, like Miep, but he too had lived in Holland for several years and was married to a Dutch woman. He became friendly with Mrs Frank and Margot and Anne, for they often visited Mr Frank at his workplace, in a busy street just behind the Dam, Amsterdam's main square.

Margot loved her new school in Jekerstraat, just a five-minute walk from home. She made new friends quickly and must have been very glad not to have to sit apart from any of the pupils because she was Jewish. Anne went to the neighbourhood Montessori school, and during her morning walk there she often met up with her teacher, Mr van Gelder, who lived nearby. Although Anne was very young, she was as chatty with adults as with children her own age. She always told Mr van Gelder the latest story or poem she had made up with her father, whom she adored.

At the Montessori school, Anne got to know Hanneli Goslar and Sanne Ledermann, who also had arrived recently with their families from Germany. Sanne lived two streets away from Anne, while Hanneli (known also as Hanne or Lies) lived on the ground floor at 31 Merwedeplein. The three girls spent a lot of time together, and Anne later wrote in her diary: 'People always said, "There they go: Anne, Hanne and Sanne."'[11]

Lies remembers that her mother brought her to school on her first day; Mrs Goslar was anxious about her daughter and how she would react to a new school. But as soon as Lies and her mother entered the building, they saw Anne, standing opposite the main doors, happily ringing the bells to call the pupils to class. Lies forgot about her shyness and rushed over to Anne, who was equally pleased to see her.

Although Margot and Anne arrived in Holland not knowing a word of Dutch, they soon picked up the language at school. At home they spoke a mixture of German and Dutch, but with their schoolfriends and teachers they only ever spoke Dutch. Mr Frank understood the language very well, but Mrs Frank, who was a housewife and didn't meet as many Dutch people as her husband and children, found it a problem. She missed her friends and family in Germany, and her old way of life there.

Margot and Anne didn't have such feelings; they were at school with friends through the day, and in the evenings and at weekends there was plenty to keep them occupied. Almost all the children in the neighbourhood knew one another, and they would meet up after school to play hopscotch, do handstands and play ball games. Anne was hopeless at handstands, but she joined in anyway. When her friend, a neighbour called Toosje, tried to comfort her by pointing out that she was shorter and younger than everyone else, Anne disagreed, saying, 'That's still no reason not to be able to do a handstand.' The girls all kept poetry albums too, in which they wrote little poems about their friends and decorated the pages with cut-out pictures. In the holidays and at weekends, friends called for each other by whistling a particular tune through the letter box. To her great disappointment, Anne could not whistle, so she sang instead: five notes up, five notes down.

For the Frank family, most of the summer of 1934 was spent visiting Aachen and taking day trips to Zandvoort, a popular seaside resort not far from Amsterdam. Mrs Frank sent a postcard to Kathi in Germany, informing her that the children were full of fun and that Anne was turning into a little comedian. Things were going well for Mr Frank too. His business was showing a good profit, and the Opekta company moved to new offices on the Singel canal, close to the colourful flower market.

For the time being at least, in Holland they were safe.

In Germany, Hitler's influence continued to grow. The Nazis saw propaganda as a weapon, and they used mass rallies, radio broadcasts and newspaper reports to promote their ideas about Jews. One of these was that the Jews were working together to take over the world and rob people of their money. The Nazis often discussed a leaflet called 'The Protocols of the Elders of Zion', an old piece of Russian propaganda that claimed to have uncovered plans by Jews to take over the world. Although a Swiss court declared 'The Protocols' to be a lie in 1937, the Nazis carried on using it to turn people against the Jews.

Spiteful untruths about Jews were published in *Der Sturmer* (*The Attacker*), the official magazine of the Nazi Party. Readers were told that Jews killed Christian children, then used their blood to make the bread eaten at Passover.* Such stories, outrageous though they were, set Jews completely apart from the rest of German society. There was no escape from propaganda; even beer mats bore the words, 'Whoever buys from Jews is a traitor.'

The state offered no protection for those hated by the Nazis. The Gestapo† had the power to arrest, question and jail anyone. In addition to the Gestapo, there was also the black-uniformed SS,‡ who also served as Hitler's personal bodyguards, the SD§ and the brown-shirted SA.

In 1935, two laws were brought in which would affect the future of all Jews living in Europe. The so-called Nuremberg Laws were set up in September 'to protect German blood and German honour'. The first law stated that German citizenship could belong only to 'a national of German or kindred blood'. The second stated that no Jew could claim to be of German blood. The laws

* *Passover*: A Jewish festival commemorating the Israelites' exodus from slavery in Egypt.
† *Gestapo*: Geheime Staatspolizei, or Secret State Police; essentially policemen, they were a group that allowed and encouraged terror as a means of keeping control of the state and its citizens.
‡ *SS*: Schutzstaffel, or Defence Guard; first the personal guard of Adolf Hitler, the SS became an army within an army. There were various branches of the SS. The concentration camps were in their charge.
§ *SD*: The intelligence and security branch of the Nazi Party.

forbade marriage and sexual intercourse between Jews and non-Jews.

The passing of these two laws helped seal the fate of six million Jews.

3

'When We Were Still in Normal Life . . .'

In her diary, Anne referred to her school years as 'ordinary life'. Despite the troubles in Germany and elsewhere, in Holland Anne and Margot could still enjoy their childhood. Omi, Uncle Herbert and cousin Stephan came to stay occasionally, and the Franks frequently visited them in Switzerland. Schoolwork was a slight problem for Anne, as Mrs Frank wrote to Kathi: 'Anne is not so well behaved as Margot and does not like to buckle down to things . . .'[12] In another letter, Mrs Frank wrote: 'Our big girl, Margot, is very hard-working and already thinks of going on to college. Little Anne is somewhat less industrious, but very droll . . . witty and amusing.'[13]

Both Anne and Margot missed some of their schooling because of illness during 1935 and 1936. Margot suffered badly with stomach aches and Anne had a weak heart. Anne's arms and legs sometimes dislocated, which didn't hurt her at all; sometimes she would do it on purpose so that she could laugh at her friends' horrified faces. Mr Frank recalled later:

Anne wasn't a strong girl. There was a particular time when she was growing quickly, and she had to rest every afternoon because of her health problems. She wasn't allowed to do any demanding sport, but had lessons in rhythmic gymnastics, which she loved. Then later she learned to ice-skate with great enthusiasm . . . Of course, she also had a bicycle, like everyone else in Holland, but she only used it to go to school, not for trips out. She preferred to stay in town than be out in the country, and she wasn't interested at all in the trips we took around Amsterdam. She enjoyed going to the beach, where she could play with other children.[14]

Anne loved to swim, and she won two medals at the public swimming pool in Amsterdam.

After school and at weekends, Anne spent most of her time with Lies (Hanne) Goslar. The Goslars were very religious and invited the Franks to share their Friday night Sabbath meal with them each week. The two families also celebrated Passover together and New Year. On Wednesday afternoons and Sunday mornings, Lies studied Hebrew. Margot also took Hebrew classes, but Anne preferred to spend Sundays with her father at his office. When Lies had finished her lessons, she went along too, and they got up to mischief, ringing each other up on the office telephones and pretending to be secretaries. Their favourite trick, especially at Anne's apartment, was throwing buckets of cold water from the high windows on to passers-by!

When Lies was later asked to describe Anne, she could only tell reporters honestly that Anne was very much typical of girls her age, although she had an obvious gift for writing. She remembers how Anne loved little secrets and loved to chat.

Anne collected pictures of movie stars, which didn't interest Lies, but they both began a collection of photographs of the children of the royal families of Holland and England, and would swap any doubles they had. Lies liked the fact that Anne was always ready to play jokes on people, and she saw that Anne liked feeling important, perhaps because Margot was always held up as an example to her. Mrs Goslar, who liked Anne very much, used to say, 'God knows everything, but Anne knows everything better!'

Anne and Lies were inseparable. They confided their secrets to each other, teased each other, shared the same dentist, called for each other with their special tune and even, in 1936, caught measles from each other; Lies was sick from 6 December and Anne from 10 December. While ill, they spoke every day on the telephone but weren't allowed to meet until they had fully recovered. On 18 December, Anne felt well enough to send her grandmother in Switzerland a short letter:

> Dear Omi, I wish you all the best on your birthday. How are
> Stephan and Bernd? Thank Aunt Leni for the beautiful ski
> gloves. Did you get some nice presents? Please write back.
> Kiss, Anne.[15]

Two frequent visitors to the Franks' home were Mr Frank's secretary, Miep, and her boyfriend, Jan Gies. Jan also lived in the River Quarter and, like Miep, he wasn't Jewish, but he was as disgusted by events in Germany as she was. He worked for the social services. On their first evening at the Franks' flat, Miep enjoyed the welcoming atmosphere and noticed a charcoal sketch of a mother cat and her kittens. The other pictures belonged to the two girls, Margot and Anne, who were clearly adored by their parents; paintings, books and playthings were scattered about the flat. The two girls ran in from their bedroom before dinner. Margot, at ten years old, was a beautiful child. She had the same hairstyle as her sister and she wore similar clothes, but she looked much neater than seven-year-old Anne, who was talkative and confident.

Anne's large circle of friends now included a number of boys. Lies remembers, 'Boys really liked her. And she always liked it a lot when all the boys paid attention to her . . . Everyone generally liked her, and she was always the centre of attention at our parties. She was also the centre of attention at school.'[16] Otto noticed the same thing; Anne was becoming 'a great talker and fond of nice clothes.'[17]

The Franks stayed in close contact with their relatives abroad. There were always birthday cards, letters and little notes, although Anne's cousin Buddy can't remember Anne's gift for writing showing up in any of those:

I had no idea she could write! I mean, I had seen her letters and so forth but she could write letters and there was nothing special in it. I never dreamed that the lively girl who visited us on holidays had the depth Anne developed [in hiding]. Margot was the serious one, always reading books and marking crossword puzzles. She was very different to Anne. I had very little contact with Margot. Not that I didn't like her, I liked her very much, but she was no fun, very quiet.[18]

Buddy looked forward to his cousins' visits to Switzerland because he and Anne were such good friends.

I adored her because she was such a good sport – always ready for fun and games. We used to dress up and play film stars. Anne had a very keen sense of fairness and justice. Whenever we got dressed up and acted out our scenes, Anne never took the best garments for herself. She always gave them to me, and the funnier I looked, the better she liked it.[19]

From 1936, all 'Aryan' Germans over the age of ten were drafted into the Hitler Youth. Each child was given a dagger bearing the words 'Blood and Honour', and had to learn to sing the Horst Wessel* song about making Germany great again and getting rid of the Jews. All members of the Hitler Youth were taught how to use a gun; when the war began, many of them joined the German army and fought for their country.

Girls also joined the German army. Elizabeth Hodl was very young when she began active service. She remembers:

With the motto, 'You are nothing, your nation is everything', an ardent nationalism was instilled in us . . . Neither I nor my friends were interested in politics. We didn't even take the time to read Hitler's book, *Mein Kampf* . . . We had been brought

---

* *Horst Wessel*: Born in 1907, Wessel was a Nazi who was killed in a street fight with Communists in 1930. He wrote the song which was named after him and which became a second national anthem for Germany.

up never to criticize or express our own opinions. At school, at home, and at work, only orders and obedience to those orders existed. We didn't realize that we were quietly and gradually being moulded to an inner readiness for war.[20]

Elizabeth eventually became involved in the peace movement.

Hitler was preparing for war. On 11 March 1938, German troops marched into Austria. They were welcomed by crowds of enthusiastic Nazi supporters in Vienna, the capital city. The anti-Jewish laws in Germany were brought into effect and thousands of Austrian Jews lost everything they owned: their businesses, their homes and their freedom. They were made to scrub the streets and clean toilets while the rest of the population and jeering Nazis looked on.

Angela Carpos, a young Jewish girl living with her mother in Vienna, recalls:

The Nazis were burning books and they came and snatched out of my hand my one and only lovely teddy bear and burned it in front of me. They didn't hit us – but what really terrified me were the scrubbings that went on. I saw neighbours and friends being humiliated, scrubbing windows and scrubbing streets. Absolute fear ran through everybody . . .'[21]

Within a year, German troops entered western Czecho-slovakia and its capital, Prague. Premysl Pitter, a Czech Protestant writer who had opened a school for poor children there, hid Jewish children in his school. When the Gestapo questioned him, he denied that the children were Jewish. Pitter and his assistant, Olga Fierz, then brought the children secretly to a refuge in the village of Myto. Together, Pitter and Fierz saved one hundred Jews during the German occupation.

The situation for Jews in the occupied countries was desperate and many wanted to get out while they could. But they were not given much help. In July 1938, representatives from a number of countries met to discuss how many Jews they were willing to take in. All the countries wanted to keep the number of refugees as low as possible, claiming that giving shelter to Jews might give rise to anti-Semitism. This reluctance to help the Jews contributed to millions of Jewish families becoming trapped when the Nazis closed the borders of the countries they occupied. It was up to individuals like Varian Fry to offer them a lifeline. Fry worked for the American Emergency Committee, a private American relief organization, and he and his co-workers in Marseille issued exit documents for Jews who wanted to leave France. After a year, Fry was fired from his job, but his actions had saved thousands, including the philosopher Hannah Arendt and artists Marc Chagall and Max Ernst.

Life for Jews in the occupied territories was unbearable. In November 1938, Jewish children were banned from attending school with Aryans and were sent to 'Jews-only' schools. Mariella Milano-Piperno, a young Jewish girl, was appalled by the news that she was not allowed to return to her school. She felt ashamed in front of the other children she knew and hated having to tell them that she wouldn't be attending classes with them any more because she was Jewish. 'Why?' she wondered. 'What did I do?' None of it made sense.

Black children and Sinti and Roma children were also thrown out of the German education system. Hundreds of them were taken away by the Nazis to be sterilized. Hannes Weiss was a nine-year-old boy at the time. He recalls:

People would yell, 'Black gypsy, dirty gypsy.' Terrible! Then the doctors came. I was just a child. They examined us, studied how you walked, measured everything, just so that they could determine what a gypsy was. We didn't know what it was all about. Later on we did . . .[22]

Among the other groups targeted by the Nazis were Jehovah's Witnesses. Elizabeth Kusserow's parents were arrested when they wouldn't give up their faith. Eventually, both her parents were released, but thirteen-year-old Elizabeth and her younger brothers got into trouble at school for refusing to salute the Nazi flag, which hung on a pole in each classroom and flew above the school building. Elizabeth felt her stomach turn when she tried to think of different ways to avoid giving the Nazi salute. She had been taught by her parents that to do it was wrong; it was the same to them as worshipping idols, which was forbidden in their religion. Elizabeth kept her mouth closed when her classmates sang Nazi songs; to her those anthems were 'horrible'.

The headmaster sent Elizabeth and her brothers away to a reform school, without telling their parents. Elizabeth's mother managed to find out where they were and convinced the principal to release them. But on the day Elizabeth and her brothers were due to leave, SS men arrived and took all three children to a Nazi training school. They remained there for six years, and were young adults by the time they saw their parents again, after the war.

During 1938, Miep and Jan often discussed politics over dinner at the Franks' apartment in Amsterdam. They all shared an intense hatred of the Nazi Party. Miep's Austrian passport had been confiscated and replaced with a German one. Mr Frank said that it was a madness that would pass, but his wife disagreed; Mrs Frank was extremely worried about the future. But all talk of politics stilled whenever Anne and Margot came into the room.

They seemed to be growing up very quickly. Miep noticed that Anne always had a bright colour in her cheeks from excitement, and she never spoke slowly but always in a rush. Margot was becoming a really pretty girl; she had a very quiet manner and always sat very straight and correct in company, with her hands folded in her lap. She was getting brilliant marks at school for her work. Anne's studies were improving too, and she was turning into a social butterfly. Miep admired how neat both girls looked – Anne's untidiness was a thing of the past now – they often wore freshly ironed print dresses with hand-embroidered white-linen collars. Both girls had immaculate hair, cut in the same dark, shiny bob. After dinner,

Anne and Margot went into their bedroom to finish their homework before Otto joined them for his evening storytelling session.

In March 1938, the Franks 'made the Viermerentocht' (a tour of the lakes), and after the holidays Mr Frank set up a second company at the offices on the Singel canal where Opekta was located. His new business, Pectacon, was listed in the Amsterdam telephone directory as a 'wholesale herb merchant, manufacturer of pickling salt and mixed spices'. Mr Frank took on a new member of staff to work as an adviser for Pectacon, Hermann van Pels. Mr van Pels had recently arrived from Osnabruck in Germany with his wife, Auguste, and son, Peter, who was the same age as Margot. Mr and Mrs van Pels were both hot-tempered, cheerful people, while their son was quiet and shy. They bought an apartment in the busy street behind the one where the Franks lived, and the two families became good friends. The van Pelses usually attended the Franks' Saturday afternoon gatherings, which were aimed at bringing German Jews together, to help them and to introduce them to Dutch people interested in their welfare.

Among the other guests was a man named Fritz Pfeffer, a Jewish dentist from Berlin, and his girlfriend, Charlotta Kaletta. Pfeffer was a very cultured man who loved sports. He had been married before and was now divorced. His young son lived in London and Pfeffer missed him greatly. Another new addition to the Franks' circle was an eighteen-year-old Dutch girl named Bep Voskuijl. She worked as a typist for Mr Frank. Tall and bespectacled, Bep was kind-hearted and painfully shy, but she got on very well with the Frank family and with everyone at

Pectacon. No one had any idea then just how closely entwined all their lives would become.

In 1938, Mr Frank took his daughters to Switzerland. Buddy remembers:

Our grandmother was living in an apartment because there wasn't enough room for her with us then. And the last time Anne was there, I remember we played at my grandmother's house with my puppet theatre. We took it in turns. Then we went to my grandmother's wardrobe and got dressed up. With hats and everything! We imitated the grown-ups – we had an awful lot of fun. We laughed ourselves sick, I remember that. She had such a sense of comedy.[23]

This was the last time Buddy ever saw Anne and Margot.

In October 1938, Hitler gave orders for 15,000 Polish Jews living in Germany to be turned out of the country. Their homes and possessions became Nazi property. The Polish government eventually agreed to take them in, but many were beaten and killed by the Nazis. One of the deportees wrote to tell his son, who was living as a student in Paris, about their treatment. After receiving his father's letter, Hirsch Grynszpan walked to the German Embassy in Paris and shot the first official he saw, Third Secretary Ernst vom Rath.

Hitler used the assassination to launch widespread attacks on Jews in Germany, Austria and the occupied part of Czechoslovakia. On 9 and 10 November 1938, 7,000 Jewish businesses were ruined, 191 synagogues burned,

91 Jews killed and 30,000 Jewish men deported to concentration camps. In Berlin, 8,000 Jews were made homeless. Nazis raided synagogues for Torah scrolls and sacred books to burn on huge bonfires, lit in the middle of Jewish neighbourhoods.

Fourteen-year-old Ester Friedman witnessed the attacks in Vienna from the window of her home:

The atmosphere up and down the street was electric; we did not know why but a feeling of fear pervaded the air. I stood by the window . . . then it happened: a crowd of brown-clad SA men, with the fearful swastika armband on their sleeves, marched down the road. I leaned out further. They entered the old people's home of the Jewish community. The windows opened and out flew books. The doors opened and out came the old people, being pushed and pulled by their beards as they could not walk quickly enough for the hordes of brown-shirted youths . . . They were made to watch their precious prayer books burn. And I watched. Buckets were brought and the ashes had to be shovelled by the old men and women. The youths and the crowds laughed at the sight. Water was brought and brushes and rags, and the old people were made to kneel and scrub the pavement. Beards were pulled until blood flowed, old women fainted – or died – I don't know. And I saw. And I smelled smoke. I turned my head and looked up the road. Our synagogue was burning – bright and high the flames roared – but I heard no fire engines.[24]

The events became known as Kristallnacht (Crystal Night) because of all the shattered glass lying on pavements in front of Jewish-owned shops. A fine of 100,000,000 German marks was placed on the Jews of Germany for 'provoking' the attack. The world's press reported what had happened and the trade boycott on German goods was stepped up, but to no effect. Jewish businesses were sold to Aryan retailers and Jews were banned from yet more public places. Panic reigned in Germany as people tried frantically to get out of the country. Some 250,000 (about half the total Jewish population) had emigrated to other lands by then, including places as distant as Shanghai.

Kristallnacht marked a turning point in the chain of events leading up to the Holocaust. After that, it was clear to everyone, Jewish and non-Jewish, in Germany and elsewhere, that the Nazis would stop at nothing in their efforts to make Germany 'Jew-free'. As a result, the British government decided to take in 10,000 Jewish children. Every western country had been asked by Jewish communities to give homes to as many children as possible, but only Britain responded. Children accepted on the *Kindertransport** had to be aged between three and seventeen, and they were expected to emigrate alone, without their parents. The usual visa entry was not necessary, but a document of identity and a bond of £50 per child was required. The young refugees would travel through Germany and Holland in sealed trains, before being put on a boat to Britain. The first group of refugees arrived in Harwich on 2 December 1938.

* *Kindertransport*: Children's transport.

Dorothy Sim, a young girl living in Hamburg, practised her English before she left:

All I succeeded in learning was 'I want to go to the WC' . . . and 'I have a handkerchief in my pocket'. Among my clothes they packed a box full of precious family photographs, my own set of cutlery and a toilet case with cloth and soap. My father had taken the toilet case with him when he fought in the First World War. He had won the Iron Cross. I recall arriving at the railway station in Hamburg. There were two stone lions guarding the entrance. I was carrying my toy dog Droll and I had my leather shoulder bag on. I dropped Droll underneath a train and a man had to climb down and rescue him. I had a peach and a pear in my shoulder bag. We children boarded the train to get our places. Then I was sent off again to say farewell to my mother and father. I can see them to this day. They were standing in a corridor behind a barrier. I said my goodbyes and then walked back up the long corridor away from them and into the train.[25]

The children were eventually either taken in by foster families, orphanages or group centres or sent to work on farms. Those children who had homes to go to in England, with relatives, friends or sponsors, went straight to London, arriving at Liverpool Street Station, where they were met by the people who would be looking after them. Most were well treated, although a few were made to work for their hosts.

Following Hitler's invasion of the rest of Czechoslovakia on 15 March 1939, a number of Czechoslovakian Jewish children were also sent to start a new life in Britain. The Nazi government at first refused to allow them transportation. An extraordinary Dutch woman named Gertrud Wijsmuller, who was already organizing the transport of refugees, managed to get them to change their minds. She took a train to Vienna to speak to Adolf Eichmann (the Nazi official in charge of Jewish emigration) and, incredibly, she persuaded him to release 600 Austrian-Jewish children. She then helped organize forty-nine other refugee transports to Britain.

The last *Kindertransport* left on 14 May 1940 when, because of the war, no more trains could pass through Holland. Only one in five of the *Kindertransport* children was reunited with his or her parents after the war.

In March 1939, Anne's Oma (her grandmother Rosa Hollander) arrived from Germany to share the apartment in Merwedeplein. Anne's uncles, Julius and Walter Hollander, had lost the family business to the Nazis, who 'Aryanized' it by giving it to someone who was not Jewish. After Kristallnacht, Julius and Walter were arrested. Julius was freed because he had been wounded while serving the German army during the First World War, but Walter was imprisoned in Sachsenhausen concentration camp, not far from Berlin. He was sent from there to a Dutch refugee camp and, after Julius was able to prove that they had the means to emigrate, Walter was released and the two of them fled to America.

Their mother, meanwhile, was happy in Amsterdam. Anne was ill with flu when Oma arrived, bringing with her a special gift for her youngest granddaughter; it was a beautiful fountain pen, wrapped in cotton wool, in a red leather case. It later became Anne's favourite pen for writing in her diary. Oma Hollander was seventy-three, but she and Anne were good friends; she could always spare time to listen to Anne's stories about school.

Mr Frank had to go abroad on business in May 1939 and, knowing how much Anne missed him when he was away, he sent her a letter which she kept 'to serve as a support to me all my life'.[26] In it, he reminded her:

I have often told you that you must educate yourself. We have agreed the 'controls' with each other and you yourself are doing a great deal to swallow the 'buts'. And yet you like to spoil yourself and like even more to be spoiled by others. All that isn't bad, if deep in your heart you remain as lovable as you have always been. I have told you that as a child I, too, often rushed into things without thinking twice and made many mistakes. But the main thing is to reflect a little bit and then to find one's way back to the right path. You are not obstinate and so, after a few tears, the laughter is soon back again.[27]

Anne later wrote about the letter in her diary (where she kept it in between the pages of the book): 'Jacque [a school friend] thought this was a declaration of love by some boy and I didn't try to enlighten her.'[28]

In the summer, Anne, Margot, Mrs Frank and Oma Hollander went on several day trips to the beach. Anne had a severe cold but insisted on going swimming. Her tenth birthday that year was celebrated with a special party to mark her entry into double figures. She invited her favourite girlfriends. A photograph taken by her father that day shows them all standing in the sun in Merwedeplein, linking arms and wearing their best dresses. Anne gave a copy of the picture to her best friend Lies, having written on the back: 'Anne Frank's birthday party, 12-6-39.'

The scramble to leave Germany was almost over, as the Nazis began to close off all avenues of escape. On 13 May 1939, the ocean liner *St Louis* left the German port of Hamburg with 930 desperate refugees on board, all hoping that the US government would allow them into the country. Although 734 of those on board had valid entry numbers (each refugee was given a number and placed on a waiting list), these did not permit entry for another three years.

The ship finally reached the Caribbean, where the refugees appealed to Latin American countries to let them in. Twenty-four refugees were taken in by Cuba; but Colombia, Chile, Paraguay and Argentina responded with a firm 'no'. The ship sailed on to Miami, where it docked for four days, waiting for a reply from the US government to the refugees' request to land. The government rejected their plea. The *St Louis* was forced to sail back to Europe.

In Belgium, scores of journalists were waiting to broadcast the story of those on board the ship. This attention resulted in Britain, France and Holland offering to take the refugees in. Gisela Knepel, on board the *St Louis* with her mother and sister, gained entry into Britain, where they began work almost immediately. Gisela found her new life hard, but did not resent being given hour after hour of housework to do. She was simply happy to have been saved. Gisela was one of the lucky ones; those refugees taken in by France and Holland had only one year of freedom ahead of them before the Nazi forces invaded, trapping them again. Of the 930 refugees who had set sail on the *St Louis*, 660 were killed in the Holocaust.

On 30 January 1939, Hitler gave a speech in Berlin in which he warned that if Germany went to war the outcome would be 'the destruction of the Jewish race in Europe'.[29] That same year, Hitler brought in the 'Euthanasia'* project, which was aimed not at Jews but at the mentally and physically handicapped. The Nazi state had always judged these people as being 'unworthy of life' and had nicknamed them 'the useless eaters'. By 1939, Hitler had decided on a solution: murder.

Nazi doctors registered all children born with disabilities, then told their parents that the children were being taken away to receive special medical attention. Most fathers were away in the German army, and those mothers who didn't believe the doctors and who tried to rescue their children were sent to work camps. Once the children were in the hands of the Nazi doctors, they were killed with lethal injections or overdoses of medicine.

---

* *Euthanasia*: The word actually means mercy killing, and by giving the project this name, the Nazis were implying publicly that they were killing these people out of compassion, when in fact nothing could have been further from the truth.

The first murders of mentally and physically handicapped children (and adults) took place in October 1939, in special hospital wards. The bodies of over 10,000 victims were burned in the crematorium of a mental institution in Hadamar. Church leaders protested against the killings, and in 1941 the project was officially called off. In reality, it went on; and it is thought that about 72,000 people were murdered in the Euthanasia project, among them approximately 5,000 children. The actual number is probably far higher.

The killing of the mentally and physically handicapped was the beginning of the end, the precursor to the Holocaust which was about to take place. On 1 September 1939, Germany invaded Poland. Two days later, the Second World War began.

4

'Good Times Rapidly Fled . . .'

The first Jews to suffer during the war were the three million Jews living in Poland when Hitler's armies invaded. About 350,000 Jews had homes in Warsaw, Poland's capital city, and another 202,220 lived in Lodz. The rest lived in Poland's other cities, towns and remote villages. Until the invasion, Polish Jews led a rich cultural life, with their own schools, hospitals, theatres, kosher restaurants, fine old synagogues and a strong sense of community.

All that came to an end on 1 September, when German forces launched a *Blitzkrieg* (lightning attack) both on land and by air, and German warships targeted the Polish Baltic coast. One month before, Hitler and the Russian leader Josef Stalin had agreed that after the invasion they would 'share' Poland. Following the defeat of the courageous Polish army, and despite the declaration of war by Britain (which had promised to come to Poland's aid), Hitler and Stalin did indeed split the country in two. German troops entered Warsaw on 30 September. Russia took control of the neighbouring states of Estonia, Latvia and Lithuania. Most of the 1,250,000 Jews living in areas ruled by the Russian government survived the war, although they were imprisoned in Soviet labour camps.

Jews living in German-controlled Poland had a very different fate. They were immediately singled out for public humiliation. Nazi soldiers cut off the beards of Orthodox Jews, forced them to perform demeaning tasks, and assaulted them in the streets. Arek Hersh, then eleven years old, lived in the Polish town of Sieradz and saw the brutality of the occupying forces first-hand. In horror, he watched German soldiers going from door to door and pulling Jewish men out into the street where they were beaten and kicked. The German soldiers shouted at the Jews to run to the marketplace, where more soldiers were waiting to attack them with their fists and boots and rifle butts. Among those men was Arek's cousin, twenty-one-year-old Idle Natal, whom Arek saw being kicked to death.

Horrific as all this was, it was just the beginning.

Mr Frank's cousin Milly, who lived in London, later recalled:

During the first months of the war, Otto was virtually our only link to the Continent. We couldn't write to relations in Germany, for England was at war with Germany. But Otto could write to Germany because he was doing so from neutral Holland. I got a letter from him saying how terribly unhappy he was because he was sure that Germany was going to attack. He said, 'I don't know what to do about the children. I can't talk to Edith about it. There's no use worrying her before she has to be worried. Forgive me, but I just had to write it.'[30]

Milly suggested that they send Margot and Anne to her in England. Mr Frank wrote back: 'Edith and I discussed your letter. We both feel we simply can't do it. We couldn't bear to part with the girls. They mean too much to us. But if it's any comfort, you are the people we would have trusted.'[31]

1940 was Anne's last full year at the Montessori primary school. From the first year to the fourth, her teacher had been Mr van Gelder. Towards the end, he noticed that Anne had a new ambition: she wanted to be a writer. Mr van Gelder was not at all surprised; he felt that she might well realize her goal. Anne's interest in writing came in useful during her last year at the Montessori school, when plays were performed. She had lots of ideas for scripts, but she also enjoyed performing. Despite being smaller than most of her classmates, she had no shyness and she liked imitating people. Her teacher at the time was the headmistress, Mrs Kuperus. She remembered Anne vividly:

Anne was a lovely girl, not conspicuous, but always active and spontaneous . . . she was intelligent, but I had more intelligent children in the class. I do know that she loved reading and drama too, she revelled in drama . . . she was a very good pupil and she took a great interest in school. She always had lots of friends, she was a girl who was easy to get on with. She had a great team spirit![32]

In his memoir written many years after the war, Anne's father looked back on his younger daughter's first school years:

She hated maths. I practised her times tables with her countless times. She only did well in those subjects that interested her, particularly history. One day she came to me and said that she had to give a short speech to the class about Emperor Nero. 'Everyone knows what's in the history books about him, what else is there for me to say?' To help her, I took her with me to a friend of mine who had a large library. There she got some specialist books, which she took home with pride. A while later I asked her about her speech. 'Oh', she said, 'my classmates didn't want to believe what I told them because it was so different from what they knew about Nero.' 'And what about the teacher?' I asked. 'He was very pleased,' she answered.[33]

In the spring of 1940 Anne and Margot began writing to two pen pals in America. The exchange was arranged by Birdie Matthews, a young teacher from Iowa who had recently visited a friend of hers (also a schoolteacher) in Amsterdam and brought home a list of Dutch children wanting pen pals. She asked her pupils to pick out names from the list. Juanita Wagner, who lived on a farm in Danville, chose Anne Frank. In her letter, she told Anne about her home life, her family and her older sister, Betty Ann, who also wanted a pen pal. Anne wrote back immediately, enclosing a postcard, photos and a letter from Margot for Betty Ann. The letters were written in English; Mr Frank probably translated them from Anne and Margot's originals in Dutch. Anne's letter to Juanita read:

Amsterdam, 29 April, Monday.

Dear Juanita,

I did receive your letter and want to answer you as quick as possible. Margot and myself are the only children in our house. Our grandmother is living with us. My father has an office and Mother is busy at home. I live not far from school and I am in the fifth class. We have no hour classes, we may do what we prefer, of course we must get to a certain goal. Your mother will certainly know this system, it is called Montessori. We have little work at home.

On the map I looked again and found the name Burlington. I did ask a girl friend of mine if she would like to communicate with one of your friends. She wants to do it with a girl about my age not with a boy.

I shall write her address underneath. Did you yourself write the letter I received from you or did your mother do it? I include a postcard from Amsterdam and shall continue to do that collecting picture cards, I have already about 800. A child I used to be at school with went to New York and she write [sic] a letter to our class some time ago. In case you and Betty get a photo do send a copy as I am curious to know how you look. My birthday is 12 June. Kindly let me know yours. Perhaps one of your friends will write first to my girl friend, for she also cannot write English but her father or mother will translate the letter.

Hoping to hear from you
I remain
Your Dutch friend
Annelies Marie Frank.

*P.S. Please write me the address of a girl. The address of my
friend is . . . [Sanne's address followed]*[34]

Juanita, Anne's pen pal, recalls: 'Needless to say, we were both
thrilled to have established communications with a foreign
friend, and we both wrote again immediately. However, we
never heard from Anne or Margot again . . . We assumed their
letters could not get through because of censorship.'[35] Juanita's
sister, Betty Ann, continues: 'We often talked and wondered
about the family. Did they have enough food? Were the bombs
dropping nearby? . . . To be very honest, we grew up in a small
country town. There were some Jewish people there but it was
no big deal. It never dawned on me that the other girls were
Jewish. If we had known, we would have prayed and done
more.'[36]

On 21 September 1939, at a secret meeting in Berlin, SS
General Reinhard Heydrich, Chief of the Reich Security
Main Office, spoke with a number of leaders of SS groups
in Poland. He kept his plans for Polish Jews secret, but
he told the SS men that he wanted vast areas of western
Poland cleared of Jews, and those Jews living in large
towns and cities were to be confined to certain districts
or 'ghettos'. Wherever possible, the ghettos – surrounded
by high brick walls and barbed wire, and patrolled by
armed guards – would be in cities where the railway
connections were good. 'So that future measures may be
accomplished more easily,' Heydrich told the SS leaders,
without further explanation.

Ghettos sprang up throughout Poland. Samuel Pisar was twelve when he and all the other Jews in his home city of Bialystok were ordered into a ghetto. After the announcement, Samuel's family gathered in the living room of their home, still in shock. Samuel remembers that it was a hot summer's day but a fire roared in the fireplace, and into it his father threw the family's most cherished possessions, such as photographs, letters and heirlooms. 'We are living our last moments in our home,' his father said. 'We don't know when we will return. We don't know who will move in here after we have gone. Each of us is allowed to carry one bag. That means the barest essentials, only what will keep us alive. Everything else must be left behind.'

Samuel protested, 'But father, what about my bicycle? And my ice-skates? And my stamp collection? And my –'

'Bicycles are not allowed,' replied his father. 'Your ice-skates will be useless. As for your stamp collection, take it along. We may be able to trade it for food. But that's all.'[37]

The largest Polish ghetto was in Warsaw, where 40,000 Jews lived, crowded and miserable. There was no privacy: families had to share one room with several strangers. Sewage flowed everywhere and starvation was rife. Children walked the streets all day, hunting for food among the vast heaps of rubbish and filth. Sometimes, those same starving children snatched food from passers-by, and even the thought of being caught and beaten did not deter them. People on the Aryan side of the ghetto watched curiously as Jewish children – often trying to feed not only themselves but their families too – took the perilous risk of running to the Aryan side when a German soldier's back was turned. Whatever scraps they might find were hidden away beneath their rags to be shared out later, among their families.

The second largest ghetto in Poland was in Lodz. Conditions were no better there, but most children still wanted to play games, to read and to learn. They had nothing, so they invented their own games. One of these involved empty cigarette packets. The children removed the bright tops of the packets and put them in a pile until they had enough to make a whole deck of cards. They played with them as if they were the real thing, shuffling them, dealing them out and arranging them by colour and name. They thought up their own games and played in this way for hours.

Several children in the Lodz ghetto are known to have kept diaries. One brother and sister, whose names have been lost, wrote a diary in the margin of a French novel. In an undated entry, the boy wrote of how his little sister had told him she had lost the will to live. She was only twelve years old. 'Will there be an end to our suffering?' the boy wondered. In another passage in the diary, he wrote that he wanted so much to live, even if only to ensure that the Nazis would be punished. 'I go on dreaming,' he wrote, 'dreaming about survival and about getting free in order to be able to tell the world . . .' Neither the boy nor his sister survived; only their nameless words remain, in that old book from the ghetto.

Even in those hopeless ghettos, parents and teachers tried to educate children. Ben Giladi was given lessons in the Piotrkow ghetto by Hela Rosenbaum, a teacher from Warsaw who shared his family's apartment. For a while Ben was the only pupil, but soon there were eight children, all sitting in the small attic room with its curved ceiling and narrow window. In the middle of the room was the table where the children sat and worked, and above the bed hung a small blackboard. It wasn't just the lessons that Ben valued, it was the sense Hela gave him and the other children of being 'equal to all the youngsters who were free'.

The children were taught literature, history, Latin, mathematics, physics and Hebrew. This was all strictly forbidden by the Nazis and so the teacher, Hela, told the children to come into class one by one, carrying their books under their clothes. Sometimes the SS appeared downstairs, and the children had to flee the attic schoolroom. In 1942, most of the pupils were sent to labour camps, Ben among them. He survived the war but his teacher, Hela, was killed by the Nazis.

Children in the ghettos also secretly put on plays, wrote stories and gave concerts. Lorraine Justman-Wissnicki, a teacher in Gorzkowice ghetto, helped children write their own newspaper. Their greatest achievement as a group was the play they performed for the entire ghetto population. It was a huge success, both for the children who sang and danced and acted, and for their audience. For the duration of the play, they had hope.

But none of the young performers, nor the crowd who applauded until their hands hurt, were to survive the war.

Thousands of Jews from the ghettos were put to work in slave labour camps. They produced everything from uniforms to hand grenades. They lived and worked in appalling conditions, in places without proper sanitation, with hardly any food and very little rest. Over half a million Jews, including many children, died while working as slave labourers.

Visiting the Franks' apartment in the spring of 1940, Miep Santrouschitz was astonished to see how quickly Margot and Anne were growing up. Margot was now a young lady rather than a girl, and she had lost the slight plumpness of her childhood to become tall and willowy. She had beautiful skin and dark, clever eyes behind her glasses. She concentrated on her schoolwork and was usually very serious. Anne admired her, despite the jealousy she sometimes felt for her elder sister, and she copied her as much as possible. Anne had developed into a skilled mimic and would imitate everyone she knew, from the teachers at school to her friends, capturing their mannerisms and voices perfectly. She loved to make people laugh and to have an attentive audience. Miep realized that Anne was going through a sudden spurt of growth; she was still very thin, but her arms and legs seemed much longer. Yet Anne remained the baby of the family and loved to get any extra attention.

The Franks went to a professional photographer, as they did every year, to record the children growing up. Anne later stuck the photos of herself into her diary. In them, she sits, hunched up, her arms folded, with her hair pinned up at the sides. She is smiling in most of them, looking above or to the side, and she captioned them: 'Things are getting more serious, but there's still a smile left over from the funny bits'; 'Oh, what a joke'; 'Whatever next?'; 'That's a funny story'; 'Nice one, as well.'[38] In one photograph she lifts her head slightly and looks deep in thought. She wrote next to it in black pen: 'This is a photograph of me as I wish I looked all the time. Then I might still have a chance of getting into Holywood [sic]. But at present, I'm afraid, I usually look quite different.'[39]

These were the last days of freedom, although Anne did not know it at the time. Hitler was planning to conquer more countries in his bid for world domination, and in the early hours of 10 May 1940, German forces invaded Holland.

5

'When the Sufferings of Us Jews Really Began . . .'

Margot Frank's best friend Jetteke Frijda remembers: 'The day after the invasion was a school day. We were called into the large assembly hall and were told that we were at war with Germany. We were sent home and didn't come back until after the surrender.'[40] Four days passed between the German invasion and the surrender of the Dutch forces. In that time, the Germans threatened to bomb the city of Rotterdam if the Dutch armed forces continued to fight. Two hours before the deadline was due, the Germans bombed Rotterdam anyway. The city was virtually wiped out, hundreds were killed and many thousands made homeless. Holland surrendered on 14 May 1940. The Dutch royal family and the government fled to London.

In a massive convoy, the Germans entered sun-drenched Amsterdam, grinning and waving from their army cars and trucks. Some 140,000 Jews lived in Holland, most of them in Amsterdam. Having read newspaper reports about the treatment of the Jews in Poland, they were understandably frightened, and many tried to escape the country, while others committed suicide. Yet at the beginning of the occupation, life went on much as it always had, apart from the air raids. Eva Geiringer[41] was a young girl who lived opposite the Franks in Merwedeplein; she recalls:

During the invasion there were aeroplanes coming over from both sides. We were terrified by all the bombing and shooting. It was the first war we encountered, and it was extremely frightening. But with the surrender, things almost became normal again. We went back to our schools and it wasn't too bad for us Jewish people or anybody else. Enough food and so on. It came gradually . . . [42]

Eva had arrived recently from Brussels with her parents and her older brother.

In August, the Franks took their usual day trips to Zandvoort. Anne had fallen in love with a fourteen-year-old boy called Peter Schiff. She later wrote of him in her diary:

Peter crossed my path and in my childish way I really fell in love. He also liked me very much and we couldn't be parted for one whole summer. I can still see us walking hand in hand through the streets together . . . I would often fetch him from school, or he would fetch me and I often went to his house. Peter was a very good-looking boy, tall, handsome and slim, with an earnest, calm, intelligent face . . . When he laughed, a naughty glint came into his eye.[43]

When one of Peter's friends teased him about Anne (she was eleven years old, three years younger than Peter), he began to ignore her. Anne was miserable at first, but her home and social life were too busy for her to stay depressed for long.

On 1 December 1940, Mr Frank's businesses, Opekta and Pectacon, moved to 263 Prinsengracht, in the pretty Jordaan area of Amsterdam. The ground floor of the building was used as a warehouse, while the first floor became offices. A steep staircase led up to the second floor, where large mixing containers, sacks of jam-making ingredients, and spices were kept. The attics above were also used for storage. Like many canal-side houses, there was an annexe at the back. The second and third floors of the annexe were not used, but Mr Frank converted the open space on the first floor into two rooms for his private office and the staff kitchen.

The Nazis had begun closing down businesses run by Jews, so Mr Frank did two things to keep his companies safe. He changed the name of Pectacon, with Jan Gies's help, to Gies & Co., and pretended that he was no longer head of the company. He did a similar thing with Opekta, resigning from the company and asking Johannes Kleiman, his bookkeeper, to replace him. In fact, Mr Frank was in charge as he had always been, and the Nazis, not realizing this, allowed Pectacon and Opekta to function as usual.

Although the Nazis had been slow to pass anti-Jewish laws in Holland at first, at the start of 1941 things began to change. In February, Jews of all ages living in Holland had to register. This was done so that the Nazis could find out exactly how many Jews lived in the country, where they were and who they were. Street violence against Jews rose sharply, and during one fight a well-known Dutch Nazi was injured and later died from his wounds. In revenge, a large group of Nazis marched into the old Jewish Quarter in Amsterdam and rounded up all the men and boys they could find, then beat them savagely before sending them away in trucks. No one knew where they had gone.

As a protest against the round-up, the Communist Party organized a strike in several major Dutch cities. For two days, trams remained in their depots, office workers stood outside in the watery sunshine, and all the harbours and steel plants closed down. Furious, the Germans threatened to punish everyone involved in the strike. Reluctantly, everyone returned to work.

The shadow cast by the Nazi occupation seemed to grow longer with each passing day. The anti-Jewish laws came in one after the other in 1941, preventing Jews from doing their jobs and enjoying a social life. The non-Jewish Dutch population in general did little to object. They were either too afraid or they did not particularly care. As a result Jews became more and more isolated.

Anne's twelfth birthday was on 12 June 1941. She wrote to Omi in Switzerland at the end of the month, explaining that she would have written sooner but her birthday celebrations had been postponed because Oma Hollander had been in hospital. She told Omi about the presents she had received, and added:

Soon we'll have the holidays. I'm going with Sanne Ledermann to a children's camp, which makes it not so lonely. Yesterday (Sunday) I was out with Sanne, Hanneli and a boy. I can't complain of a lack of boyfriends. We don't have much chance to get tanned any more because we can't go to the swimming pool [this was one of the anti-Jewish laws]. It's a pity, but that's how it is.[44]

Anne went to summer camp with Sanne, as she had told her grandmother. Her father, mother and Margot joined her there in July. When they returned home, Miep and Jan announced that they were getting married. Everyone was invited, but Oma Hollander was seriously ill with cancer, and Margot also had an illness of some sort. Edith Frank stayed at home to look after them, but Anne attended the wedding with her father. She had a new suit and a matching cloche hat with a ribbon for the occasion. Her hair, which had grown quite long, was once more cut into a neat bob and she looked every inch the chic young girl her friends admired. The weather was fine, and a street photographer took snaps of the wedding party. The following day, Mr Frank gave a reception for the couple at the Prinsengracht offices. Anne and Bep Voskuijl prepared the food and acted as waitresses. When Miep and Jan visited the Franks at their home soon afterwards, Miep noticed that Anne had a new interest: boys. She still talked about the cinema and which famous film-stars she liked best, but now she chatted about the boys she found attractive and whom she thought liked the look of her too. Miep was happy to listen to Anne talk, but could not help feeling that the war was speeding up Anne's development. On the outside Anne still looked like a young girl, but inside there was a part of her that was 'suddenly much older'.

*   *   *

A new law brought in that summer ordered the separation of Jewish children and non-Jewish children in school. Anne and Margot, together with all the Jewish children at their school, were called into a special assembly. They were told that they would have to transfer to the new Jewish school. Anne wept when she had to say goodbye to Mrs Kuperus, the headmistress. Later, Otto Frank recalled how, under the new law,

it was very difficult for Anne and Margot to keep up their friendships with non-Jewish children, particularly now that it was forbidden for Christians to visit Jewish families and vice versa . . . When I think back to the time when a lot of laws were introduced in Holland, which made our lives a lot harder, I have to say that my wife and I did everything we could to stop the children noticing the trouble we would go to, to make sure this was still a trouble-free time for them.[45]

Anne and Margot were transferred to the Jewish Lyceum, a three-storey building with a long concrete playground in front and one at the back. An archway at the front led through to the Amstel River. Laureen Klein, a friend of Margot, remembers seeing Anne at the tram stop every morning, now that they had changed schools: 'We lived two stops beyond the Franks. Anne and her entourage would get on the street car and I would think, "Isn't she lively?" She definitely was the centre of the circle. Talk, talk, talk.'[46] Anne went into the first form of the Lyceum with Lies Goslar, and Margot went into the fourth with her best friend, Jetteke Frijda.

Anne found a new best friend at the Lyceum, Jacqueline van Maarsen, who also lived in the River Quarter. The two girls became very close, and they found that they shared many of the same interests and could spend hours sitting on the flat roof of Anne's apartment, chattering about all kinds of things. They even organized film shows together, sending out tickets to their schoolfriends, who were then invited to Anne's home to watched a rented film on the old projector. Jacqueline remembers,

Anne made everything fun. I have never met anyone else since then who enjoyed life as my friend Anne did. Anne was the one with the movie-star collection [postcards], and I helped her with it. When we stayed at each other's house, it was Anne who decided about that. We alternated – not every night of course, just sometimes – but Anne always invited herself. She was pretty too. The photograph that everyone knows – where she sits at a desk with her arms folded – isn't her best picture. She had a brace on her teeth then and was trying to hide it. She looked much nicer than that.[47]

Although Anne sometimes complained about her mother and sister, Jacqueline thought that they were 'always very sweet to Anne and patient with her . . . Margot was very nice to Anne always. She really was "the big sister". I suppose I looked up to her, like my own sister. Margot was very clever, but I don't think I really noticed that then. I never saw any rivalry between them. Margot was always very nice to Anne, and Anne wasn't always nice, but she was never unpleasant with Margot.'[48] Anne never complained about her father, but then the two of them were similar. Jacqueline remembers: 'Otto was an extrovert, just like his daughter Anne . . . She always had to have someone around to talk to or play with or else she became bored.'[49]

Just after Jacqueline and Anne first met, Mr Frank took Anne out of school for a couple of days to go on a short trip to Arnhem. He sent a postcard to his mother from there on 14 September 1941:

Dearest Mother, Anne and I have travelled here for a couple of days, the others stopped in Amsterdam. We're not staying long, I just wanted to have a bit more peace and quiet, but didn't want to go off completely on my own. Anne is always good, dear company and she was able to have a few days off school. Everything is well. All our love to everyone, yours Otto.[50]

The front of the card showed their hotel, the Groot Warnsborn, and across it Anne wrote happily: 'We're staying here! In the middle of the forest! Isn't it wonderful?'[51]

When Hitler's forces invaded Russia on 22 June 1941, right behind the troops were the *Einsatzgruppen*, specialist Nazi soldiers whose main task was to murder as many Jews as they could. They entered towns and villages, rounding up the Jews, then took them out to forests or ravines to shoot them. Sometimes local people would help the *Einsatzgruppen* with these murders. The victims were buried in mass graves. At a place called Babi Yar, just outside the city of Kiev, over 30,000 Jewish men, women and children were killed by the *Einsatzgruppen*. Afterwards, Jewish slave labourers were forced to burn the bodies to hide all evidence of the crime. Another 8,000 Jews who had been in hiding and imprisoned in slave labour camps were also killed at Babi Yar. The largest number of Jews killed by the *Einsatzgruppen* was at Drobitsky Yar, where over 40,000 people were killed.

By now, German forces also occupied Denmark, Norway, Holland, Belgium, Luxembourg, France, Romania and Yugoslavia. The *Einsatzgruppen* in Russia had proved so successful in their task that Hitler felt certain his secret plans for Jews in the other countries under his control could now become reality. In March 1941, Heinrich Himmler told his men: 'The Fuhrer has given the order for a final solution to the Jewish question and we, the SS, must carry out that order.'[52]

But it wasn't until early the following year that the plans were fully explained to the Nazi officials who would be in charge of carrying them out. Hitler's 'Final Solution' – the extermination of every Jewish man, woman and child in Europe – was presented to fifteen senior Nazi and German officials at a top secret meeting on 20 January 1942, at a villa on the shores of Lake Wannsee, close to Berlin. Among the men there that day were Adolf Eichmann (Head of the Gestapo's Jewish affairs section), and Heinrich Müller (Head of the Gestapo). All were gathered there on the orders of Reinhard Heydrich, who described how the 'Final Solution' would take place and what he expected of the men sitting before him. He told them that in order to ensure the destruction of the Jews in Nazi-occupied territory, 'Europe will be combed from east to west'.[53] Eventually, these plans would include Jews living beyond Nazi control; Adolf Eichmann handed round a paper listing countries (among them England and Ireland) and the number of Jews living in each one. When the meeting was over, Eichmann, Heydrich and Müller sat by the fireside, drinking cognac and smoking cigars.[54]

What the fifteen officials were told that day in the villa at Lake Wannsee was this: Jews would be shipped from every country under Nazi control to special camps, where they would be murdered. Throughout Germany and much of Poland, concentration camps for forced labour already existed. Under the 'Final Solution', these camps would take on a different role, new camps would be built, and almost every prisoner entering the camps would be killed. Experiments in murdering large numbers of people had already taken place before the meeting at Lake Wannsee, in a camp called Auschwitz.

Auschwitz lay close to the small Polish manufacturing village of Oswecim, where the Sola and Vistula rivers entwine in marshy, barren tracts of land. Auschwitz was the name given to it by the Germans, who chose it for its easy rail access; Auschwitz was a main junction, connected to all the European capitals. But it was also an isolated spot. Thirty convicted German criminals were sent to Auschwitz on 30 May 1941 to serve as *kapos*.* Together with 300 local Jews, they began to prepare the site.

Rudolf Höess became Commandant of Auschwitz on

* *Kapos*: Head prisoners who acted as guards.

29 April 1941 and remained there until 1943. In the summer of 1941, Adolf Eichmann visited the camp to talk to Höess about killing techniques, including murder by gas. Heinrich Himmler also called on Höess to tell him about the 'Final Solution', adding that 'Auschwitz would serve as the centre of destruction'.[55] At the end of the meeting, Himmler confided, 'Every Jew that we can lay our hands on is to be destroyed now.'[56]

On 3 September 1941, some 300 Jews and 900 Russian prisoners of war were taken to a cellar in Auschwitz. They were gassed using Zyklon B, the trade name of a chemical used in pest control: tiny blue-green crystals that dissolved on contact with the air, releasing a deadly gas. The crystals were dropped in through vents in the ceiling of the gas chamber. There was no possibility of survival.

After the meeting at the villa on Lake Wannsee in 1942, instructions for enlarging the main camp at Auschwitz were given. The building of Birkenau, the camp's killing terminal, started in September. Birkenau was situated across the railway line from the main camp. There were many sub-camps within it: a women's camp, a men's camp, a Gypsy camp, medical huts, etc. There were also gas chambers, undressing rooms, crematoriums and pits where bodies could be burned. Electrified barbed wire surrounded the camp, with towers where armed guards constantly kept watch. Later, it was enlarged again. Seven Polish villages were destroyed and two thousand people were deported to make space for Auschwitz II. Auschwitz III consisted of the surrounding sub-camps and factories dealing in everything from coal mining to agriculture.

Jews living in the Polish ghettos were the first to be deported. They were rounded up and put on trains, travelling under the impression that they were being resettled for work in labour camps. In the Warsaw ghetto, where starvation was rife, Jewish families were lured to the death camp of Treblinka with the promise of something as simple as bread and jam. Most concentration camps were fitted with gas chambers. Told that they were being taken into showers or to be disinfected, the innocent people were led into the chambers.

The diary of David Rubinowicz, a young boy deported from Poland, has survived. David began keeping his diary in 1940. In 1942 he wrote about the order to 'evacuate', which meant all Jews in his town were to be deported. Earlier that day as he stood outside, watching the wind tear through the fields, making the grass surge back and forth like the sea, he saw the village watchman putting up a notice. David went over to see what it said and spoke to the watchman who told him about the forthcoming evacuation. When he arrived home, David told his family about the notice. Everyone had the same questions: where would they end up?

David's diary ends abruptly as he is discussing the murder of two Jewish women: 'They went out into the woods and shot them there. The Jewish police immediately went to bury them in the cemetery. When the cart returned it was full of blood. Who . . .'

David was deported to Treblinka. He died in the gas chambers there, shortly before his fifteenth birthday.

In general, there were few children in the concentration camps. There were two main reasons why this was so: children could not work as hard as adults, and they represented the future of the Jewish people. In most camps, selections were made immediately after the trains pulled into the compounds (usually at night, to confuse the exhausted passengers). The old, the sick, pregnant women and children under the age of fifteen were almost always sent straight to the gas chambers. Teenagers who managed to convince SS officers that they had a trade (for example, that they were trained electricians) were allowed into the camps along with those who appeared to be fit enough to work. But even among the workforce in the camps there were regular selections for the gas chambers. In Auschwitz, where approximately one million Jews died, Dr Josef Mengele, the SS officer in charge of making the selections on the railway ramp, chose a number of children for his so-called 'medical' experiments. When he no longer needed them, the children were sent to the gas chambers.

In January 1942, Oma Hollander died. Anne and Margot were devastated by their grandmother's death, and Anne later wrote in her diary: 'No one will ever know how much she is in my thoughts, and how much I love her still.'[57] She missed her grandmother's support; Oma Hollander had always been able to calm the often difficult relationship between Anne and Mrs Frank.

In April 1942, the Franks celebrated Passover with the van Pels family. Otto Frank's thoughts were on the future. In a letter written many years later, he explained,

I soon realized that the time would come when we would have to go into hiding to escape the deportations. After having discussed the matter thoroughly with Mr van Pels, we came to the conclusion that the best solution would be to hide in the annexe of our office building. This would only be possible if Mr Kleiman and Mr Kugler would be willing to take full responsibility for everything connected with our hiding, and if the two secretaries of the firm [Miep and Bep] would co-operate. All four immediately agreed although they were fully aware of the dangerous task they would take upon themselves in doing so. By Nazi law everyone helping Jews was severely punished and risked being put into prison, being deported or even shot. During the following months we prepared the hiding place.[58]

The annexe was thoroughly cleaned out and cleared of rubbish. Food, bedclothes, soap, towels and kitchen utensils were easy to move. Furniture and other large items were picked up in a van owned by Mr Kleiman's brother and taken to the hiding place after office hours. All work done in the annexe took place gradually, at weekends and in the evenings. Paper was pasted over the windows in the front house facing the annexe, shielding the rooms from the warehousemen and visitors to the office. The families would move in at some time in July 1942.

Anne and Margot were not told immediately about the hiding plan; their father wanted them to enjoy what was left of their freedom. Children in general did not worry as much as their parents did. In her diary, Anne writes, 'Jacque used to say to me, "You're scared to do anything because it may be forbidden."'[59] But today Jacqueline remembers, 'We talked about the laws as they came in, but not very much. The worst thing was not knowing what was going to happen next. All the time, there were new regulations, but you just got used to them.'[60]

During Easter 1942, Anne discovered her bicycle had been stolen. Since Jews were banned from using public transport, her only option was to walk everywhere. She now had a half-hour's walk to school each day. The evenings were no longer restful either, because British aeroplanes on their way to bomb Germany flew over Amsterdam every night. When the air-raid alarm sounded, everyone living in Merwedeplein gathered together at the arched entrances to the apartments. Searchlights criss-crossed the sky and anti-aircraft guns boomed and flashed. Everyone was frightened. There was a man called Dr Beffie who lived nearby and who would join them during an air raid, always with a piece of bread in his hand. He ate very slowly, and Anne always stared at him. Then one night, as the all-clear sounded, Anne turned to her young neighbour Toosje and said, 'Good heavens, if I chewed so slowly, I think I'd be hungry all my life!'

Anne gave this time the title 'Do You Remember? Reminiscences of My Schooldays' in her book of short stories, written in the confines of the annexe. She mused, 'That one year in the Lyceum was sheer bliss for me; the teachers, all they taught me, the jokes, the prestige, the romances, and the adoring boys.'[61] Otto noticed his daughter was becoming even more popular as she grew up:

She was always on the go, and always brought a whole community of children with her wherever she was. People loved her because she had ideas, what to play, where to play, some new things to do . . . Anne had one quality that was a bit annoying. She was constantly asking questions, not only when we were alone, but also in the presence of others. When we had visitors, it was very difficult to get rid of her, because everyone and everything was of interest to her.[62]

Anne, Lies, Jacqueline, Sanne and Ilse Wagner (Lies's best friend from the Lyceum) formed a table-tennis club that summer called 'The Little Bear Minus Two'. Jacqueline recalls, 'We formed the ping-pong club because there was so little we were allowed to do, and also, children were not spoiled with choice like they are now.'[63] The odd name came about by mistake. They wanted to name the club after a constellation of stars, and they thought that the Little Bear had five stars (like their group), but later they discovered that in fact it had seven, hence the 'minus two'. Mini-tournaments were held in the dining room of Ilse's home with her ping-pong set. Afterwards, being 'very partial to an ice-cream', they would visit the Oasis ice-cream parlour or the Delphi tea room, both in the River Quarter. Jacqueline explains: 'We never sat inside Oasis. The Jewish boys and girls from the neighbourhood congregated there, but it was a social encounter, played out on the pavement. One bought an ice cream and went outside to eat it . . . We always ran into people we knew there. Anne loved walking behind boys and fantasizing that they were all her admirers.'[64]

In May 1942, Anne wrote to congratulate Buddy on his seventeenth birthday. She told him, 'I've been busy every day. This evening I won't get home until ten, but I'm usually escorted home by a young man. How's it going with your girlfriend, the one you sent a picture of? Please write more about her, things like that always interest me. Margot also has a boyfriend, but he's even younger than mine.'[65] Margot sent her own birthday greetings to their cousin, writing, 'I said to Mummy yesterday how well I remember seeing you on Omi's birthday when we were ten years old. Hopefully we'll see each other before you're eighteen . . . I don't think it's so nice to have your birthday on a weekday because you have to go to school all day, and now, next year, we will both have finished school. But who knows what will happen then . . .'[66]

6

'It's an Odd Idea for Someone Like Me to Keep a Diary . . .'

On 29 April 1942, Jews living in Holland, France and Belgium were subjected to a new law which made them more visible than ever: the forced wearing of the Jewish Star of David. The German announcement in the press instructed all Jews in public to wear the star, which was made of yellow material, black-bordered and six-pointed, 'the size of a palm'. In the middle of the star was the word 'Jew'. It was to be worn on outer clothing on the left-hand side of the body, and Jews were not allowed to wear any other form of decoration or insignia. Jews in Germany and Czechoslovakia had been wearing the star since September 1941. Stars could be bought only from distribution centres and cost four cents and a stamp from the clothing ration card.* Refusal to wear the star resulted in a fine or imprisonment – and even Jews in jail had to wear them. Only children under the age of six or twelve (depending on where they lived) were exempt.

---

* *Rationing*: During the war, food and clothing were rationed. Everyone was given a ration book with stamps in it which had to be handed over to the shopkeeper whenever an item was bought.

Livia, a young Jewish girl living in Hungary, was outraged at the idea of having to wear the star. She wrote in her diary that she simply would not do it. It was a 'horrible, horrible thing' and the idea that her school-friends would see her with the star affixed to her clothing made her feel as if she would die of shame. To avoid wearing the star, Livia stayed indoors for a week. Her mother pleaded with her, telling her in a gentle voice that it was only a star, it did not kill or condemn or harm. 'It only means that you are a Jew,' her mother said, and surely Livia was proud of that? Livia didn't know if she was proud. She had never had to think about it before. But she did know that she hated being marked like a piece of cattle.

In Holland a slogan was coined: 'Wear It with Pride, the Yellow Star!' Some Jews were proud of their star, but others were ashamed. When they were first issued, some non-Jews, outraged at this latest anti-Jewish law, wore them in protest. The Gestapo threatened them with deportation. The Nazis did not make idle threats, as an event in June 1942 made clear.

That month, SS chief Reinhard Heydrich was murdered in the Czechoslovakian city of Prague. In revenge, the Nazis made an example of one community. On the evening of 9 June 1942, SS troops stormed into the village of Lidice, thirteen miles from Prague. The men of Lidice were marched to a barn, where they were shot. Some were no more than fifteen years old. Seven women who had refused to leave their husbands were also killed. The rest of Lidice's population – 196 women and 105 children – were driven in trucks to the nearby town of Kladno. The SS burned Lidice to the ground. From Kladno, the women were sent to Ravensbruck concentration camp, and most of the children were sent to Germany to be trained as good Nazi children. Those children whose blood was not 'pure' enough for this were gassed. Only seventeen of Lidice's 105 children were traced after the war. Most of the women survived, but none of them ever saw their children again.[67]

Elsewhere, a rash of new anti-Jewish laws made life almost unbearable for those caught in the Nazi web. Eva Geiringer, whose family were neighbours of the Franks, recalls:

People always say nowadays, why did you do this and why did you do that, but we were so scared. We thought, if we do the things that are demanded of us, we'll be all right. You're told to have a 'J' on your passport, you go and do it. Especially in a smaller community like Amsterdam, where everybody knows who is Jewish and who comes from where. We thought, if we wear the star, if we obey the curfew, if we do everything, nothing will happen to us.[68]

Fifteen-year-old Esther van Vriesland, also living in Holland, began keeping a diary in 1942. That summer she wrote about the endless list of regulations and how it would surely affect her holidays. She no longer looked forward to the last day of school. Each new law made her feel more miserable than the last. The humiliation of having, as a Jewish girl, to stand up on the tram when everyone else could sit down, was almost too much to bear. 'Will it never end?' she wondered.

For Esther, as for so many, it did end, though not as she had hoped. Esther was deported that summer and died in the gas chambers at Auschwitz. The last line of her diary read: 'Please, let me write about peace in the next notebook.'[69]

Friday, 12 June 1942 was Anne's thirteenth birthday. Her father took her to Blankevoorts, a large bookshop around the corner from her house, to choose a present. Anne picked out a diary – actually a red-and-white-checked autograph album – from the books and stationery on sale. Lies arrived early that morning to collect Anne for school and admired the diary briefly before Anne put it away in her bedroom. In the sitting room, all Anne's other presents were on display and there were flowers everywhere. In the kitchen, her mother was baking a strawberry tart, while her father sat comfortably in his chair and shared a joke with Lies as usual. When it was time to leave, Mrs Frank gave Anne a basket of sweet biscuits to hand out at school, and Anne added some biscuits she had made. In the afternoon, Lies, Jacqueline, Sanne and Ilse gave Anne their joint gift, a book called *Tales and Legends of the Netherlands.*

At some point on her birthday, Anne wrote in the diary for the first time. She pasted in a school photograph of herself from winter 1941 with the caption, 'Gorgeous photograph, isn't it!!!!' At the front of the book she wrote, 'I hope I shall be able to confide in you completely, as I never have in anyone before, and

I hope that you will be a great support and comfort to me.'[70] All Anne's friends were aware that she had been given a diary. Lies remembers Anne writing in the check-covered notebook at school, holding her hand over the page so that no one could see what she had written. Jacqueline agrees: 'We were very curious about it . . . we wanted to see what she had written about us.'[71] She also remembers Anne had an unusual way of writing: 'Anne always wrote with her pen between her index finger and her middle finger because she had sprained her finger at some point. I had always admired her handwriting and tried to imitate it by holding my pen the same way.'[72]

Anne's party was held on the Sunday after her birthday, and Jacqueline's strongest memory of the day is of Anne's happiness at being surrounded by her friends: 'With sparkling eyes she had watched her friends enter and opened her presents expectantly. She had enjoyed being the centre of attention.'[73] Lies recalls the gaggle of children in the apartment; Anne's parents handing out slices of strawberry tart on china plates; glasses of cool milk for everyone; Margot and Jetteke Frijda joining in with them all; the blinds being pulled down as Mr Frank set up the projector and then Rin Tin Tin and the Lighthouse Keeper whirring into life on the blank wall. Lies also remembers having to leave the party early to help her mother with her baby sister, Gabi, and her feelings of jealousy when she saw Anne and Jacqueline whispering together. She thought of that moment in the months that followed and always told herself, 'If I'd known what was going to happen, I wouldn't have minded.'

By the end of June, Anne had a new boyfriend, Hello Silberberg. Hello was also from Germany and had arrived in the River Quarter in 1938. He lived with his grandparents and was a handsome sixteen-year-old when his cousin introduced him to Anne. He remembers, 'She was very attractive and she liked to laugh and to make people laugh. She was very entertaining and extremely lively. She did little imitations of people that were very clever. In my memory I always see her sitting in a big chair, with her hands under her chin and looking directly at whomever she was with . . . I think I was probably in love with her. She seemed to think so too.'[74]

Anne's parents liked Hello, but his grandparents disapproved of her: they thought she was too young for him and they didn't like the fact that Hello had left his previous girlfriend for her. Anne worried about this and questioned him about their future together. He told her, 'Love finds a way!'

At the end of the school year, the children received their examination results. Margot's were excellent as usual, and Anne's were better than she had expected, although she and Lies would have to resit the maths exam in September. Around this time, Mr Frank told Anne about the hiding plan. Margot already knew, and Anne confided in her diary her impassioned hope that 'the fulfilment of these sombre words remain far distant yet'.[75]

Although she had no way of knowing it then, Anne paid her last visit to Jacqueline and her family during the first week of July, when she arrived at the van Maarsens' flat on Hunzestraat to show off a new dress. Mrs van Maarsen told her that it looked very sweet on her. Anne smiled and replied, 'Why, of course it does. It's brand new.'

The morning of Sunday, 5 July 1942 was sunny and hot. Anne's father walked to the Jewish hospital in town to visit some of the elderly patients there, leaving Anne and Margot at home with their mother. Hello called around to make arrangements with Anne for an outing later that afternoon. When he had gone, Anne stretched out on the terrace to read. At three o'clock the doorbell rang and there was a call from the street, 'Miss Margot Frank?' Mrs Frank went down to answer it. A policeman handed her a registered envelope.

Inside was a card ordering Margot to report to the SS the next morning.

At the end of June 1942, Adolf Eichmann had informed all departments involved in the 'Final Solution' that from July 1942 mass deportations to the extermination camps in the East would begin.

The Nazi government decided to deport 4,000 Jews in Holland to 'German work camps'. The first call-up notices were sent out to German Jews on Sunday, 5 July 1942. The notices didn't explain where they were going or what they could expect; all that was included was a list of clothing to be taken in a rucksack. The Jewish Council in Amsterdam urged people to obey the call-ups, fearing what might happen if too many resisted, and tried to reassure those targeted that in the camps they would be put to work, 'ordinary relief work', nothing more sinister than that. Most of those receiving the call-up on 5 July were German Jews, like Margot, aged fifteen or sixteen.

If the people receiving the call-up notices did not report as ordered, then the Nazis would simply pick Jews to be taken away at random. Often Nazis barricaded neighbourhoods while all the houses were searched for Jews. Dotje Cohen, who was very young and was living with her foster-parents, heard the street being closed off by German soldiers. The windows of her home were suddenly filled with white light as spotlights were turned on to the apartments. Her foster parents picked her up quickly, strapped her to a mattress and then closed her in a cupboard in the hope that she would not be discovered by the Gestapo. 'Don't make a sound,' her foster parents told her, and from inside the cupboard Dotje remained silent, listening as the boots of the soldiers came closer up the street. She heard them bang on the outside door, and then they came up the stairs, right into the room where she was hidden and flung open the cupboard door. They saw only a mattress, not realising that Dotje was strapped to its underside. She heard them leaving.

But later, the Nazis came back for Dotje and broke into the house, shouting her name. They pushed aside her foster-father, who tried to fight them, and found Dotje. One of the soldiers pushed her down the stairs. When they dragged her out into the night air, Dotje didn't even feel the cold; sheer terror took over, numbing her senses. Dotje survived, but she never forgot the fear she felt that night.

In Holland, Jews were either sent straight to the railway station for deportation or to the Hollandse Schouwburg, an old theatre close to the city zoo. Below its ornate ceilings, Jewish men, women and children lay slumped on the floor for days, some dying of thirst and hunger. There was no fresh air and only dull, artificial light. In the foyers, the stalls, the balconies and the corridors, children screamed and wept. Older people walked about as if in a trance, waiting for the moment when the trams would come for them and they would be driven, in full view of the rest of the Dutch population, to the station and, from there, to the camps.

Ironically, the terrible conditions in the theatre led to over 1,000 Jewish children being saved. The theatre was so overcrowded that the Nazis decided to send the children to stay in the Jewish nursery directly across the street. The director there, Henriette Rodriquez-Pimentel, and the young Jewish women who worked for her, rescued as many children as they could. Although newcomers to the nursery had to be registered by the Jewish Council, all the files on the children were destroyed by nursery assistant Walter Süsskind and Felix Halverstad, who worked at the Council. The children could not be traced. They were then smuggled out of the nursery in several ways. The nursery assistants would take toddlers and older children out on walks and then meet a member of a Resistance* group, who would bring them to safety. Babies were secretly carried out in rucksacks, potato sacks and laundry baskets. Next door to the nursery was a teacher training college whose director, Professor van Hulst,

---

* *Resistance*: People opposed to the Nazi regime who worked together secretly against it. They forged documents, found hiding places for those who needed them, smuggled out reports on what was happening in the country to those in the free world, and sometimes killed Nazi officials.

also wanted to help. Children were dropped carefully over the wall of the nursery into the garden of the college, where someone would be waiting to take them to a safe address. One of the children saved by the nursery staff later became the Mayor of Amsterdam, Ed van Thijn.

Jewish children were not the only ones to be deported, although they formed the largest group of children sent to the concentration camps. The second largest group of children in the camps belonged to Roma and Sinti families. In 1940, all Roma and Sinti families still living in Germany had been sent east to Poland to live in ghettos there. When the mass deportations of Jews from the ghettos to the death camps began, Roma and Sinti were also included. After the war, it was estimated that approximately half a million Roma and Sinti had been killed in the camps – almost the entire Roma and Sinti population of eastern Europe.

Throughout 1942 and 1943, the deportation trains rolled out of Europe's major cities. There was only one way to avoid the dreaded transport, for all other avenues of escape had long been closed: to go into hiding.

As soon as Margot received the call-up, Mrs Frank left home to tell the van Pelses that the hiding plan would have to be brought forward. At first, Margot told Anne that the SS had sent a call-up for their father, but then she told her the truth. Anne began to cry. Hello returned at the same time as Mrs Frank and Hermann van Pels. He was told that Anne couldn't see him just then, and Jacqueline was told something similar when she telephoned later. Anne and Margot were sent to their room to begin packing. Anne put her diary and old letters into a satchel. They were more important to her than clothes. She still did not know where their hiding place would be.

Anne's father returned from visiting friends at five o'clock. When he was given the news, he called Mr Kleiman, who came over immediately. Miep and Jan Gies called round to take the Franks' belongings – mostly clothes and toiletries – to their own home for safekeeping until they were in the hiding place. An atmosphere of panic and fear made everyone much quieter than usual. The Franks' lodger, Mr Goldschmidt, called on them that evening. He knew nothing of the hiding plan. He stayed until ten o'clock, and an hour later, Miep and Jan returned to take away more items and clothing.

When they had gone, Mr Frank wrote to his family in Switzerland, hinting that they were going into hiding: 'We are all well and together, that's the main thing. Everything is difficult these days, but you just have to take some things with a pinch of salt. I hope we'll find peace this year already so that we can see each other again. It's a pity we can no longer correspond with you, but that's how it is. You must understand.'[76] Anne added her last greetings: 'I cannot write a letter about the holidays now. Regards and kisses from Anne.'[77]

It was half past eleven when they went to bed. Anne was exhausted and fell asleep instantly.

It was raining the next morning when the family ate breakfast in semi-darkness at 5.30 a.m. They each wore as much clothing as possible, to lessen the amount they had to carry. Margot filled her satchel with schoolbooks and pulled out her bike to wait for Miep, who arrived at six o'clock on her bicycle. They rode off across Merwedeplein silently. Mr and Mrs Frank left a letter for the lodger, asking him to take Anne's cat, Moortje, to their neighbours. They left the beds unmade and scattered the breakfast things on the table as if they had had to leave suddenly. At 7.30 a.m. they set off on foot in the warm rain. The streets were dark and cars sped by, their headlights blurred by the downpour. As they walked, Anne's father told her about the hiding place.

Margot and Miep were the first to arrive at the annexe. Margot was on the verge of passing out, so great was her fear of discovery. Miep gripped Margot by the arm, feeling that Margot was soaked to the skin, just as she was. Miep pushed her gently through the door to the annexe and went back downstairs to take her place in the office. She shook the rain from her coat and sat in her chair, her heart thumping.

When Anne and Mr and Mrs Frank reached the building later that morning, drenched by the rain and tired by the long walk, they went straight upstairs to the annexe. Margot was waiting for them.

The annexe was a mess, with boxes and sacks piled up everywhere. In Mr and Mrs Frank's room were two divans, three tables, bookshelves, a built-in cupboard and 150 cans of food. A window overlooked the courtyard below and the houses opposite. A door to the right led to Anne and Margot's narrow room. It had a window, two divan beds and three built-in cupboards. Next door was a washroom with a lavatory. A doorway on the right led back into the passageway and to the entrance door. On the floor above was a large room with double windows looking out on to the courtyard again. This was set aside for Mr and Mrs van Pels. It was almost bare, apart from a sink, some cupboards, a gas stove, two beds and a table. Another door led into the tiny damp room where Peter van Pels would sleep. There was a small shuttered window facing the front house, and the stairs to the attic were in the middle of the room, along with a bed and a cupboard. From the arched side window in the attic, the tower of the Westerkerk (West Church) could be seen.

Visiting the annexe later that day, Miep found Mrs Frank and Margot lying on their beds in despair, but Anne and her father were busy trying to get things organized as quickly and quietly as possible. Miep could not imagine how they must have felt, but she was upset to see her friends forced to leave behind their home, their possessions and their other friends. By then, the Franks' neighbours in Merwedeplein knew that they had gone. They heard the rumour – spread by Mr van Pels – that the Franks had escaped to Switzerland, taken there by a German officer whom Mr Frank knew from the First World War. Everyone was glad for them.

No one was surprised, because other families that had received the call-up notice had also disappeared. But Anne's friends were very upset when they heard; Lies and Jacqueline went straight round to Anne's apartment and spoke to the Franks' lodger, Goldschmidt, who had spread the rumour of the family fleeing to Switzerland after finding a letter deliberately left by Mr Frank, hinting that this was what had happened. Jacqueline asked Goldschmidt whether they could have a last look around Anne's bedroom. He shrugged, and let them in. Jacqueline and Lies walked around the room in a daze, not speaking. Jacqueline remembers seeing 'Anne's unmade bed and on the floor in front of it, her new shoes, as if they had just been kicked off . . . I saw Variety, the game she had just got for her birthday and which we had played like crazy the past few weeks, just lying there . . .'[78] They found Anne's swimming medals and took them; a few small reminders of the friend who had vanished.

7

'We Have to Whisper and Tread Lightly . . .'

Approximately 100,000 children were hidden during the war. Every situation was different: some children hid alone, some with their families and some with strangers. They hid in the countryside and in cities. Some were hidden by a single person, some by a network of people. Occasionally a child decided to go into hiding or on the run after their parents had been taken away in the round-ups. But generally the arrangements to go into hiding were made by parents or guardians. It was unusual for an entire family to go into hiding together as the Frank family did; it seemed safer to separate, and it was easier to hide a single person than a group. A young child hiding alone could be passed off as a visiting relative or war orphan. For the child, this usually meant no contact at all with their real families; they were given new names and sometimes a new religion, and they were completely dependent upon the person caring for them.

Hiding places varied enormously, from city apartments above busy workplaces (as was the case with Anne and her family) to barns in the remote countryside. Hania Goldman[79] hid with her mother and sister in a Polish hayloft after her father was shot by German soldiers. The farmer, who was a woman, let them stay but gave them no help at all. Hania was able to go outside only on those nights when there was no moon, since it was dark under the trees then. Hania and her family spoke to each other in hushed whispers for two and a half years, remaining hidden in the loft. But no matter how bad things got or how terrified they were, Hania never considered giving in.

The sewers of Warsaw provided five-year-old Krystyna Chiger and her family with a hiding place. They managed to live there – in the wet and the dark – with several other Jews, large reddish-coloured rats and yellow worms that crawled over the stones beneath their feet. Non-Jewish sewer workers provided them with food and water. The people in hiding tried to avoid the rats, which spread disease and ate their bread. But Krystyna's little brother, Pawelek, loved the rats. To him, they were pets and he shared his food with them. One of the other women hiding in the sewer cooked soup and coffee and offered some to Krystyna and her family. During the day, as water seeped down the walls, Krystyna listened to the cars driving on the street above them. She could hear people talking and children laughing and playing. She longed to join them. Miraculously, Krystyna and her family survived, though at first her brother did not want to go up into the daylight; he preferred the darkness of the sewer, which was the only home he remembered.

Wherever the hiding place itself was, the shock of being forced to actually go into hiding was enormous. It meant leaving behind all one's belongings and way of life, loved ones, friends, community. Eva Geiringer, who hid with her mother while her father and brother found a separate hiding place, explains:

You couldn't imagine what it was like to go into hiding. Not to go out and see people – that's something that, as a child, you can't grasp. But when we actually went into hiding, that's when it started to sink in. I was very lively, I was thirteen and had so much energy, but I just couldn't do anything. I was very afraid and very upset. I used to have wrestling matches with my mother to get rid of my energy. It was very, very hard.[80]

Nothing and nowhere was safe; the smallest mistake might lead to discovery. In some houses, a second hiding place had been built in case of a raid by the Nazis. Children had to hide behind false walls in wardrobes, under floorboards, in mice-infested attics. The most normal and basic activities became a problem when hiding; in her diary, Anne Frank writes of being able to flush the toilet only at certain times, when they could be sure there was no one else in the building. If people who visited the host family didn't know there was someone hidden in the house, then the child had to be doubly careful. They were frightened, confused and often terribly lonely.

Many children found refuge with religious institutions.

They had no contact with their families and had to pretend to belong to the community where they were housed. Being forced to reject their own religion was something many older children found disturbing. Gisele Naichouler Feldman, then eleven years old, found shelter with the Catholic children's sanatorium in Chavaniac, France. It was difficult for her to pretend to be a Catholic, to sing in the choir and attend church each Sunday. She had to memorize the prayers and explained any mistakes by telling those in charge that her parents were not very religious. Her strange life made her feel like a fraud, and 'pretending to be someone I was not' gave her enormous feelings of guilt.

Some children felt guilty, but they understood that their safety depended upon their ability to blend in with the other children. Andy Sterling, a young Hungarian boy, was sent by his parents to hide in a Catholic orphanage. He arrived at the same time as another boy called Paul. The two of them were taken into an office where the priest and his assistant told them not to tell a soul that they were Jewish, and not to talk to each other about it either. The priest went through the morning prayers with them, then showed them to their dormitory. Andy lay there, petrified, desperately longing for his parents. In the morning he went along to the services and copied everything the other boys did. But when they crossed themselves, Andy felt uncomfortable; it was something he had never expected to do. Eventually, he crossed himself, and soon it became a ritual. His fear overcame his guilt.

When the area was bombed, the pupils moved into the bunker for safety. They survived until liberation, and Andy was one of the few Jewish youngsters in hiding to be reunited with his family. Later, he discovered that there had been six other Jewish boys hiding in the orphanage, besides himself and Paul.

Apart from the emotional difficulties of going into hiding, one of the most common practical problems was food. Resistance organizations forged ration books for people in hiding who could not obtain them legally. As the war went on, certain foods became scarce, and during the Hunger Winter of 1944–5 in Holland (when the Nazis cut off all electricity supplies and food could no longer be brought into the cities), some Jews in hiding died of starvation or illness. It was impossible to carry out the corpse normally; in several cases when a fugitive had died, the body was put inside a mattress, to be taken out without arousing suspicion. Sometimes, in Amsterdam, bodies of Jews who had been in hiding and had died were to be seen floating in the canals.

Discovery was the greatest fear, but being in hiding was also incredibly dull for normally active children. They passed the time painting, drawing, reading, writing or studying. Gerry Mok was six years old when he was taken out of Amsterdam to hide in the Dutch town of Hoorn in February 1942. Like other hidden children, he changed address many times to avoid capture, and in some places his host family started to teach him how to read and write. Gerry responded eagerly, keen to go on with his lessons. Soon he was reading anything he could lay his hands on; it was a way of escaping reality, and he lived 'partly in a dream world' through books.

Eva Geiringer was given lessons by her own mother while they were in hiding. She remembers: 'From the time Mutti and I went into hiding, I entered a seemingly protected world. My days were spent entirely in the company of my mother and I remember them as full of warmth and love. During the next two years, hidden in our attic, she taught me German, French, geography and history . . .'[81]

Bertje van Rhijn, hiding in the Dutch town of Kampen with her family, was glad that the old lady who had agreed to shelter them had kept all her children's books, as well as their toys and games. Bertje discovered schoolbooks, atlases, novels and biographies and she read them all. The old lady was also a member of her local library and borrowed books for her hidden guests. Bertje also kept a diary.[82] Writing in a journal was also a way of preventing boredom.

Moshe Flinker, another hidden child, used his journal to work out his opinions, his ambitions for the future and the thoughts and feelings he preferred not to share with his family. Moshe was born in The Hague on 9 October 1926. His father was Polish but had emigrated to Holland, where he became a successful businessman. When the Flinkers received their call-up notice in July 1942, they went into hiding in Brussels, across the border in occupied Belgium. There was no record of the family living there; they were able to hide 'openly', using false identity papers.

In November 1942, Moshe began to keep a diary. His religion was important to him and he tried to understand the events unfolding around him in relation to God. On 26 November, he worried about other Jews who had lost their faith: 'They will think that there is no God at all in the universe, because had there been a God, He would not have allowed such things to happen to His people.'[83] Moshe, on the other hand, found that his belief in God gave him strength: 'Had I not religion, I would never find any answer at all to all the problems that confront me.'[84] In July 1943, he wrote: 'I shall never stop hoping, for the moment I stop hoping I shall cease to exist. All I have is hope; my entire being depends upon it.'[85]

Moshe's diary ended in September 1943. A few months later, the Nazis raided the apartment where the Flinkers lived; they had been betrayed by a well-known Belgian collaborator. Moshe and his family were taken to Malines, the Belgian transit camp, and from there to Auschwitz, where he and his parents were gassed upon arrival. His brothers and sisters survived the war and, when they returned to their old apartment in Brussels, they found Moshe's diary and had it published.

Not all children in hiding had paper on which to write, or books to read. Some didn't have the energy or the will to occupy themselves in this way; they were made to work by their host families in the house or, if they lived in the countryside, on a farm. The difference in backgrounds between the hidden child and the host family also frequently created problems: children whose parents were avid readers might be placed with a family who saw studying as wasteful when there was 'real' work to be done; or the host family could be deeply religious and try to influence the hidden child into converting from Judaism. Although many hosts were kind and loving to the children they took in, some were not, acting out of greed and hoping to extract a lot of money from the parents of the child they were hiding. Generally, the younger the child, the better the chance that the child and his or her host would bond. Older children could not forget their real parents and the lives they had led before the Nazis took away their freedom.

After the war, Jewish children who had been in hiding did not always want to go back to their real parents, if they had returned. These children had grown attached to their foster families, and some were too young to remember their real parents. They suffered again when they had to leave their foster families and return to their real families. Often their foster families did not want them to go back, which resulted in a battle for the child. Parents returning from the concentration camps sometimes found it difficult to get used to being with their children again after all they had gone through. Some parents were unable to trace their children who had been placed with strangers or who had moved from hiding place to hiding place. In those cases, children sometimes stayed with the people who hid them; many did not even know that they were

Jewish and that they had parents who had been killed in the concentration camps.

In all, eight people hid in the secret annexe at 263 Prinsengracht: Anne and her family, the van Pelses and, from November 1942, the dentist from Berlin, Fritz Pfeffer. They had to be extremely careful that no one else, apart from their helpers, knew they were there. The door to the secret annexe was concealed by a special bookcase that could be moved by those who knew where to look for its hidden hinges. Windows were covered with strips of thick material and blackout boards, used by everyone during wartime to confuse enemy bombers. There were certain rules that had to be strictly observed: the eight in hiding had to be as quiet as possible during office hours; the curtains were to be kept closed; the toilet was out of bounds when anyone else was in the building, and so on. Their fears of discovery were made worse by a number of burglaries that occurred at the offices during their period in hiding, and by the arrival of a new member of staff in the warehouse who became very curious about what was going on in the building.

Apart from their fears of being discovered, their biggest worry in hiding was food. Every morning, Miep and Bep gave the families their rations, which they collected on their behalf. Bread was bought from a friend of Mr Kleiman, and a friend of Mr van Pels provided them with meat. Miep visited a grocery shop nearby for vegetables and became friendly with the owner, who was in the Dutch Resistance. He soon guessed the reason for Miep's frequent visits to his shop, but he never gave away her secret. Bep was responsible for the milk ration, and she smuggled several bottles a day from the office supply to the annexe. She also provided fruit for her friends in hiding when prices were low. The attic quickly became a food store: potatoes, peas and other vegetables were kept there, along with lots of tinned foods. In her diary, Anne sometimes grumbles about the lengthy food 'cycles' they had to endure – weeks when only one or two types of food were available to them. As the war dragged on, Miep often spent hours queuing for groceries, only to be told when she got to the counter that there was nothing left. Several major arguments broke out in the annexe over the poor food and the way it was divided.

There were other practical difficulties. Soap, for example, was hard to find in the shops, and Miep or Bep had to give them whatever they could spare from their own rations once the original supply had dwindled. Washing was not a problem, since there was a basin in the annexe, but taking a bath proved a little more difficult. Privacy was the main concern; each person chose his or her own place, using a portable tin washtub. Anne and Margot occasionally used the front office after hours, but they had to wash themselves in semi-darkness so that no one passing by in the street would see them. Electricity had to be used sparingly because when their rations ran out they were left without light or warmth. In that situation they had to use candles to enable them to see and to pile coats on the beds at night to ward off the cold. When it was dark and they had no electricity, they amused themselves and kept warm by exercising and dancing. Illness was another cause for alarm because they could not call a doctor. In the winter of 1942, Anne had a high fever, brought on by influenza, and all kinds of potions and remedies were used to cure her.

Being cramped in a few small rooms with no chance to escape affected them all. Squabbles broke out over minor matters and relationships grew extremely strained. Most of the arguments were about food, but other things also caused trouble. Mr and Mrs van Pels had some furious rows about money, while Mrs Frank and Mrs van Pels argued endlessly about bringing up children. Mrs van Pels and Anne also had numerous quarrels, usually over Anne's 'cheekiness'.

Despite the fear, the practical problems and the frequent arguments, there were also many humorous moments in hiding. Hermann van Pels loved to tell jokes, and Anne and Peter enjoyed dressing up in their parents' clothes for a giggle – Anne in her father's suit, Peter in one of his mother's dresses. Any cause for celebration was welcomed in the annexe. Birthdays, religious festivals, good news about the war, and so on – all were greeted with enormous pleasure. The helpers often joined in the celebrations and even threw a surprise party in the annexe at the end of 1942 to welcome in the New Year. Such occasions made life a little easier to bear.

Everyone in hiding tried to keep themselves as quietly busy as possible through the day: studying, sewing, writing, reading. To her annoyance, Anne wasn't always allowed to read the same books as Margot and Peter, but she loved biographies, mythology and romance. She compiled family trees and studied shorthand with Margot and Peter. Mr Frank made sure that the three teenagers didn't miss out on their education, and he tutored them in a variety of subjects, including languages, algebra, geometry, geography and history. The attic became a peaceful spot for study. Anne also used it as a writing room, and Peter made himself a carpentry workshop in one corner. After her lessons and at night, Anne sometimes relieved her boredom by borrowing her father's binoculars and zooming in on the houses opposite the courtyard. Past the black skeleton of the chestnut tree, she could see a dentist's surgery where the patient one evening was an elderly woman who was 'awfully scared'.[86]

In her diary, Anne compared being in hiding to being on holiday in a very strange hotel. She tried to be brave, but at night fear often got the better of her, and the silence made her imagination run wild. The minutes crawled by and each creak and movement made her wonder if they had been discovered. Planes flew past, firing at the enemy in the dark, and she felt sure that the annexe would be hit by a bomb. Night-time terrors aside, she often wrote about how lucky she felt to be in hiding with people she knew, cared for by friends. She became really downhearted only when she thought about her old life, her friends and her cat, Moortje, whom she missed very much. She wrote then how miserable she was:

When someone comes in from the outside, with the wind in their clothes and the cold air on their faces, then I could bury my head in the blankets to stop myself thinking: when will we be granted the privilege of smelling fresh air ... ? Cycling, dancing, whistling, looking out into the world, feeling young, to know that I am free – that's what I long for . . .[87]

She escaped into daydreams of 'after the war', but found that the best way to overcome her fears and sadness was to go up into the attic where the window was open. There she could gaze at the sky and the tower of the Westerkerk. Staring at the chestnut tree, 'on whose branches little raindrops shone, at the seagulls and other birds that looked like silver in the sun',[88] brought her peace for a while.

The helpers tried to protect their friends from the reality of life on the outside, the deportations and the cruelties, but it was impossible to keep everything secret. Besides, the people in hiding wanted to know the truth, however bad it was. They listened to the radio regularly and heard reports on the Dutch station, Radio Oranje, of Jews being killed by shooting and being poisoned by gas. They tried hard to keep their spirits up, despite the horror of it all, by keeping to their routine and burying themselves in work and hobbies. Anne wrote sensibly in her diary:

It won't do us any good or help those outside to go on being as gloomy as we are at the moment . . . Must I keep thinking about those people whatever I am doing and if I want to laugh about something, should I stop myself quickly and feel ashamed that I am cheerful? Ought I then to cry the whole day long? No, that I can't do . . .[89]

The persecutions made them more aware of their Jewish identity than ever before. Of the eight in hiding, Pfeffer was the most religious, but they all observed the major festivals, enjoyed traditional Jewish food when it was available, and welcomed in the Sabbath every Friday night. Anne's interest in her religion increased as she got older. She had nightmares about the fate of other Jewish people, and in her dreams she saw her friend Lies dressed in rags, starving and crying for help. For Anne, Lies became a symbol of Jewish persecution, and in her diary she wrote how wicked she felt to be sleeping in a warm bed while her friends were suffering: 'I get frightened when I think of close friends who have now been delivered into the hands of the cruellest brutes the world has ever seen. And all because they are Jews.'[90]

Anne frequently became upset about other things too, including her relationship with her mother. The two had many rows, which were largely the result of the pressures of being in hiding and Anne's need for independence (she felt that her mother treated her like a baby). Anne's father did his best to keep the peace between his wife and daughter, but in the end it was Anne herself who learned to have more patience with her mother and to try to see things from her viewpoint for a change.

Being in hiding did not prevent Anne from taking care of and pride in her appearance. She pin-curled her hair in the same style as Margot, and she made a combing-shawl out of rose-patterned material, which she tied under her chin to catch stray hairs when she brushed out her curls. She dreamed of being able to buy lots of make-up and clothes after the war, writing in her diary a long list of what she thought she would need. She studied her face in the mirror and asked Margot whether she was attractive (Margot told her she had nice eyes!). From time to time, everyone tried to make a real fuss of her; the helpers brought her new shoes and the cinema magazines they knew she loved, in order to spoil her a bit. They knew that it was very difficult for a lively and sociable young girl to put up with the quiet and loneliness of life in hiding. Early in 1944, she noticed that Peter was becoming more interested in her, and when he looked at her she was happy and excited. Soon he was confiding in her, which was exactly what she wanted. They spent hours in the attic together, sitting by the window and looking out at the Westerkerk or across the courtyard, and watching winter turn to spring on the chestnut tree. However, gradually the intense feelings Anne had for Peter began to fade; he could not satisfy her need to talk about 'deeper' subjects, and he wasn't as intelligent as she was.

In 1944, Anne wrote at length in her diary about how she had changed since her birthday in 1942. She now felt that she was a young woman, one who wanted things that were different from the lives led by the other women she knew, something more than a husband and a family (although she wanted those too): 'Although I'm only fourteen, I know quite well what I want, I know who is right and who is wrong, I have my opinions, my own ideas and principles, and although it may sound pretty mad from an adolescent, I feel more of a person than a child, I feel quite independent of anyone . . .'[91] She sometimes found it hard to be optimistic but, with a struggle, she succeeded: 'It's really a wonder I haven't dropped all my ideals, because they seem so absurd and impossible to carry out. Yet I keep them because, in spite of everything, I still believe that people are really good at heart.[92]

When the deportations began, rumours about the 'work camps for Jews' started to spread. In leaflets written by Resistance organizations, attention was drawn to the gassings in Poland, and the BBC Home Service – which Anne listened to from her hiding place – carried reports of Jews being '. . . regularly killed by machine-gun fire, hand grenades – and even poisoned by gas'.[93] Most people did not believe these reports. But many of those who did, and who were appalled by what was happening, decided to resist.

Like the people whom they hid, all rescuers were different: they were rich or poor, religious or atheist, with families or without. Some saved those whom they knew, others saved strangers. Their common bond was the courage to act, in the knowledge that the punishment they faced was imprisonment, deportation or death.

What motivated them? Marian Pritchard, a rescuer in Holland, was moved to help after the scenes she witnessed during her morning bicycle ride to school. Her route took her past a Jewish children's home. As she neared the building, she saw that a truck had pulled up outside the school and that German soldiers were throwing children into the truck. She watched in horror as babies and children up to the age of eight were taken by an arm or a leg or by the hair and tossed into the vehicle. Marion felt herself trembling and crying with fury. Two other women rushed forward to help the children but the soldiers merely heaved them into the truck as well. Marion sat on her bicycle, enraged and sickened. 'That was the moment,' she later recalled, 'that I decided that if there was anything I could do to thwart such atrocities I would do it.'

Apart from all practical matters, such as providing a hiding place, food, warmth and security, helpers had to be supportive of the people whom they hid, who often didn't see anyone else other than their rescuers. Miep Gies recalls: 'I never felt the desire to be free of the Frank family. It was my fate, my burden and my duty.'[94] In an interview, when asked if she was ever afraid, Miep replied:

No, especially not at the beginning . . . caring for those people was the main thing. Sometimes I lay awake at night and thought, 'Oh those poor people hidden up there, how awful. How would I feel?' . . . We, the helpers, were aware that occasionally there were difficult moments for each one of us, but we didn't talk about it. Everything had to take its course, and if you were to talk about it you'd begin to feel a certain pressure. You'd spend the day thinking about the people in hiding, and that couldn't happen. We had to appear as relaxed as possible to the rest of the world, otherwise people would become suspicious.[95]

In her diary, Anne Frank pays tribute, not only to Miep and the other people who hid her family, but to all rescuers:

It is amazing how much noble, unselfish work these people are doing, risking their own lives to help and save others. Our helpers are a very good example . . . Never have we heard one word of the burden which we must certainly be to them, never has one of them complained of all the trouble we give. They all come upstairs every day, talk to the men about business and politics, to the women about food and wartime difficulties, and about newspapers and books with the children. They put on the brightest possible faces, bring flowers and presents for birthdays and Bank Holidays, are always ready to help and do all they can. That is something we must never forget; although others may show their heroism in the war or against the Germans, our helpers display heroism in their cheerfulness and affection.[96]

Although most helpers worked alone, there were also whole communities who came together to save Jews from deportation. In Denmark, when the Germans announced their plans to deport all Jews, the king and the heads of the Danish churches objected, and Danish universities shut down so that the students could help in the rescue effort. The deportations were due to take place on the night of 1 October 1943. The population, forewarned, moved into action. No fewer than 7,906 Jews were taken to ports, where Danish sea captains and fishermen took them on board their boats and sailed them to safety in neutral Sweden. The Germans, enraged, started to hunt for any Jews who had been too old or sick to travel; they found 500 and sent them straight to Theresienstadt (originally a ghetto, later used as a holding camp, with no gas chambers). But still Denmark did not forget: every month, the Danish authorities asked for an update on their condition and insisted that they must not be harmed. Aware that they were being watched, the Nazis did not ill-treat them. Of the 500 Jews from Denmark who had been deported, 423 survived the war.

One of the most famous cases of 'desk rescue' comes from Hungary. After the Nazi invasion of Hungary in 1944, Raoul Wallenberg, a 32-year-old Swedish banker, issued 630 Swedish visas to Hungarian Jews, and his colleague Charles Lutz issued 700. Working on behalf of the American-based War Refugee Board, Wallenberg was also able to give homes to 15,000 Jews in a number of apartments funded by the Board. The passes he had issued gave the Jews the protection of the Swedish government. The Nazis were furious and arrested 80,000 Jews in Budapest. They were marched into Austria under conditions so terrible that almost half of them died. Wallenberg followed the survivors and gave out protective passes so that they could return home. In the meantime, the Nazis issued orders for the 70,000 Jews living in the Budapest ghetto without passes to be killed. Wallenberg contacted the SS general in charge of the executions and told him that he would be hanged as a war criminal if the murders went ahead. The SS man decided not to carry out the order.

Wallenberg continued to help Jews until January 1945, when Russian troops entered Budapest. He was last seen driving to the Russian commander's headquarters to discuss saving the city's remaining Jews. He was arrested by Russian soldiers and imprisoned in Moscow on suspicion of spying for the Americans. Wallenberg was never heard of again.

In Kovno, where more than 30,000 Jews had lived before the war, 200 children were saved by Lithuanians who hid them in the city and the surrounding countryside. A twelve-year-old orphan called Sima led the Jews out of the Minsk ghetto into the Russian forests. Her youth, her blonde hair, wide blue eyes and sweet face deterred the Nazis from suspecting her. A Resistance fighter who worked with Sima recalls:

No assignment was too difficult for Sima. Before going out on a mission she listened carefully to the given instruction, then she would repeat what she was told, trying hard not to miss a single word. Her small pistol was always in the special pocket sewn into her coat. Before starting out she would always point at it and say, 'Don't worry, the Fritzes [Germans] will not take me alive.'[97]

Sima survived the war.

Even some young Germans were determined to speak out against the Nazis. Hans and Sophie Scholl, brother and sister in a large, politically active family who despised Hitler, didn't hide Jews, but they were disgusted by what was happening to them. Hans and Sophie attended Munich University where, together with a small group of friends, they formed the White Rose resistance group. Their methods were pacifist: they wrote and distributed leaflets urging people to take a stand against the Nazis, and especially the anti-Jewish measures. Soon their actions came to the attention of the Nazis themselves, who became determined to find the leaders of the White Rose group.

On 18 February 1943, Hans and Sophie started distributing the latest White Rose leaflet, in which they had written of their delight about the German defeat in Russia. The university caretaker saw them and had them arrested. Sophie and Hans were taken to the Gestapo headquarters in Munich. They refused to betray anyone, but other members of the group were soon arrested. Hans and Sophie's parents tried desperately to secure their release, but the Scholls and one other member of the White Rose, Christoph Probst, were sentenced to death. Their parents visited them in jail before they were executed. When Mrs Scholl began to weep, Sophie told her brightly, 'It's only a few years' life I'll miss!' That evening, Hans and Sophie were executed by guillotine. As Hans walked to his death he shouted, 'Long Live Freedom!' Other members of the White Rose were also executed. A few days after Sophie and Hans's burial in south Munich, graffiti appeared on walls throughout the town. It read: 'Their spirit lives.'

Despite their own personal freedom being severely limited, many Jews were also active in the Resistance. In 1943, the Nazis announced their plans to deport the remaining inhabitants of the Warsaw ghetto. On the morning of 19 April, German soldiers entering the ghetto

Otto Frank with Margot and Anne, August 1931.

Anne and Margot, 1933. This photo was taken during their stay in Aachen with their grandmother.

Anne's tenth birthday, June 1939, including Anne (second from left) and Sanne Ledermann and Hanneli Goslar (third and fourth from left).

Hans Massaquoi, aged seven.

Hitler Youth, parading through Nuremberg in 1938, salute
Adolf Hitler.

A synagogue in
Berlin burnt down
by the Nazis on
Kristallnacht in
November 1938.

Kindertransport children arriving in England from Germany in December 1938.

Anne and Margot at the beach in Zandvoort. Anne is eleven years old in this photo.

Jewish children on a tram in the Warsaw ghetto in Poland, 1940.

Anne at her writing desk in their house in Merwedeplein, 1941.

Adolf Hitler and Nazi Chief of Police, Heinrich Himmler, watching Stormtroop manoeuvres, 1941.

A child in the Warsaw ghetto warns others of the approach of Nazi gangs, 1942.

Anne's friend, Jacqueline van Maarsen.

Eva Geiringer, aged thirteen, a few weeks before she went into hiding with her mother.

Moshe Flinker, aged sixteen, was betrayed and sent to Auschwitz.

(*Below*) Jewish women and children arrive at Auschwitz concentration camp, 1943. Many were sent immediately to the gas chambers by Dr Josef Mengele.

Otto Frank's office with Victor Kugler (left), Bep Voskuijl (front, middle) and Miep Gies (right) who helped the Frank family during their time in the Secret Annexe.

A white rose lays on the grave of Sophie Scholl, a young German who founded the White Rose resistance group against the Nazis.

Hannah Senesh, aged fifteen, at her home in Budapest, Hungary.

Peter van Pels, who was in hiding with the Frank family.

Young prisoners at Dachau concentration camp cheer the American troops who liberated the camp in May 1945.

were attacked by gunfire and grenades made from petrol-filled bottles. Stunned by the Jews fighting back, the soldiers immediately retreated. The following day they returned, and broke into the Jewish hospital, where they shot all the patients before setting fire to the building. Despite this, ghetto fighters continued to attack Nazi soldiers entering the compound for a whole month. The ghetto fighters had just two machine guns and fifteen rifles; the Nazis had 135 machine guns and 1,358 rifles.

In the end, the Nazis set fire to the ghetto. Some 7,000 Jews were killed; 56,000 captured. Those who had been captured were either killed immediately or sent to death camps. Four months later, on 1 August, when Polish forces fought against the German occupiers, those Jews who had managed to survive the ghetto emerged again to do battle with their enemies. The Germans brought this uprising to an end on 2 October. A few Jews found new hiding places in the rubble of the destroyed city.

On some level, Jewish resistance occurred in every country; for instance, in Holland a group of Jews calling themselves the Palestine Pioneers helped people to escape the country. Their headquarters was a farm near the village of Loosdrecht, where one of the organizers, a non-Jew named Joop Westerweel, worked with a German-Jewish refugee, Joachim Simon. Most of the people they rescued were able to reach Palestine, but both Westerweel and Simon were captured by the SS and executed.

One of the most famous cases of resistance by Jewish women is that of Hannah Senesh, who was born in

Budapest, Hungary, in 1921. Hannah's father was a
playwright, and both her parents were interested in politics
and culture. She never thought about what it meant to be
Jewish until she experienced discrimination at school.
Afterwards she became a committed Zionist and left
Budapest for Palestine in September 1939. Hannah
volunteered to serve in the British military during the war
and was parachuted into Yugoslavia on a secret mission
to Hungary. As she crossed the border into Hungary she
was captured by the Nazis, who imprisoned her in her
home town. She was twenty-two years old when she was
killed by firing squad. Shortly before she was put to death,
she wrote a poem in her prison cell:

> One – two – three . . .
> eight feet long,
> Two strides across, the rest is dark . . .
> Life hangs over me like a question mark.
>
> One – two – three . . .
> maybe another week,
> Or next month, may still find me here,
> But death, I feel, is very near.
>
> I could have been
> twenty-three next July;
> I gambled on what mattered most,
> The dice were cast. I lost.

[Budapest, 1944][98]

Despite the efforts of rescuers and Resistance workers – many more than are mentioned here – a large number of those who went into hiding were betrayed. In Holland, the *Police Gazette* published lists of Jews who were missing, calling for their capture. The Nazis tried to fool the Jews in hiding by taking out a public notice telling them to give themselves up and promising that they would not be deported. It was a lie. The Nazis also employed people to hunt out Jews, and they offered money to anyone who could tell them where Jews were hiding. In Holland, an infamous group of men called the Henneicke Column captured hundreds of Jews. At first their wages were low, but as time went on and fewer Jews were found (most of them having been deported), betrayers were given a pay rise to encourage them to work harder.

People who were not actually employed by the Nazis to betray the Jews but who did so anyway had different reasons for making phone calls or writing letters to the authorities about hidden Jews. Some were anti-Semitic or had a personal grudge against a particular Jewish person, while others acted out of malice or because they thought they should obey the law. In Holland, approximately 9,000 of the 25,000 Jews who went into hiding were arrested thanks to informants. Their hiding places were ransacked by the Nazis, who took anything of value, either to keep for themselves or to send back to Germany.

Discovery was never very far away. Every month during 1942 and 1943, some 12,000 Jews were deported from Holland. They included those who had been betrayed in hiding and those who were taken in the mass round-ups. On 20 January 1943, a train left Holland bound for Auschwitz, carrying over 1,000 Jewish adults from the Apeldoorn home for the mentally ill, and seventy-four boys and twenty-four girls from the nearby home for seriously physically and mentally handicapped children. With the children were the nurses who had always cared for them; they had been told that they could stay with their patients or start new jobs in a very modern home for the mentally ill 'in the East'. The nurses chose to stay with the children. Upon arrival at Auschwitz, everyone on board the train was sent straight to the gas chambers.

The last large-scale raid in Amsterdam took place on 29 September 1943. Approximately 5,000 Jews were arrested. Afterwards, the only Jews still living in Holland were those married to non-Jews, those with fake identity papers and those who were in hiding.

Anne's diary was a great comfort to her, just as she had hoped it would be. She usually wrote in it in her parents' room or her own room, or at a desk by the window in the attic. Everyone in hiding knew that Anne was keeping a diary because she often asked them not to disturb her while she was writing, and she sometimes read aloud from it, though no one ever tried to read it without her permission. When the original diary which her father had bought her was full, the helpers gave her office ledgers and sheets of loose paper to write on. In the summer of 1943, Anne began to write short stories. Some of these, such as 'The Battle of the Potatoes' and 'Villains!', are essays about the daily routine in the annexe. 'Villains!' concerned the problem of fleas in the annexe during the summer months, although the villains were not the fleas, but the van Pelses, who had ignored the advice they had been given on how to get rid of the tiny pests, resulting in an outbreak of itchiness. Other stories, such as 'Kitty' and 'Eva's Dream', are more like fairy tales. Anne kept a record of all her non-diary work in an oblong office cashbook, providing an index and details about when the stories were written. Sometimes she read aloud from this book to her companions and the helpers.

At the start of 1944, Anne was already thinking about what would happen to her diary after the war: 'I trust to luck, but should I be saved, and spared from destruction, then it would be terrible if my diaries and tales were lost.'[99] Her writing, she felt, was the finest thing she had, and she now knew what she wanted to do when the war was over and she had completed her education:

I want to write later on, and even if I don't become a writer I won't neglect my writing while doing some other job. Oh yes, I don't want to have lived for nothing like most people. I want to go on living after my death! And therefore I am grateful to God for giving me this gift, this possibility of developing myself and of writing, of expressing all that is in me.[100]

On 28 March 1944, Anne was listening to Radio Oranje, broadcast from London. A speech by the Dutch Minister for Education, Art and Science urged people to keep safe all their personal documents, such as diaries and letters. When the war was over, these would be placed in a special centre, so that future generations could learn how ordinary people had lived. The other occupants of the secret annexe immediately turned to Anne and began talking excitedly about her diary. Anne herself was thrilled by the idea and began rewriting her whole diary with a view to publication. On 11 May, she started work properly on the task of adapting her diary into a book she wanted to call Het Achterhuis (The House Behind). The new version was written on sheets of coloured carbon paper. Anne altered parts of what she had originally written, deleted some details, added others and combined a number of entries. She drew up a list of name changes for everyone she had mentioned, calling herself 'Anne Robin'. On 12 June 1944, Anne turned fifteen and, as a present, Miep and Bep gave her a collection of unused office ledgers in which to write. Anne then asked Bep about the possibility of sending her stories off to magazines under another name. When Bep asked her if she really wanted to be a writer, she said, 'Yes . . . no . . . yes . . .' then answered with a sudden, brilliant smile, 'No, I want to marry early and have lots of children!'

Two months later, on 1 August, Anne wrote her last letter to Kitty, the name she had given to her diary. She ended it:

. . . if I'm quiet and serious, everyone thinks it's a new comedy and then I have to get out of it by turning it into a joke, not to mention my own family, who are sure to think I'm ill, make me swallow pills for headaches and nerves, feel my neck and my head to see whether I'm running a temperature, ask me if I'm constipated and criticize me for being in a bad mood. I can't keep that up: if I'm watched to that extent, I start by getting snappy, then unhappy, and finally I twist my heart around again so that the bad is on the outside and the good is on the inside, and keep on trying to find a way of becoming what I would so like to be and what I could be, if . . . there weren't any other people living in the world. Yours, Anne M. Frank.[101]

Early on the morning of 4 August 1944, a telephone call was made to the Gestapo headquarters in south Amsterdam. The caller told officials that there were eight Jews in hiding at 263 Prinsengracht. At half past ten that same day, four members of the Gestapo raided the Secret Annexe.

8

'I Am Afraid of Prison Cells and Concentration Camps . . .'

Whether they were discovered in hiding or were picked up during one of the mass raids, Jews were usually sent first to a transit camp in the country of their capture. The transit camps were miniature concentration camps without gas chambers. They were in remote areas, away from major towns or villages, surrounded by high barbed-wire fencing and patrolled by armed guards.

Upon arrival, newcomers were registered and made to hand over their possessions. They were searched for hidden valuables and then told which barracks they would be in. Most transit camps let families stay together during the day, but at night men and women were separated. There were daily roll-calls (*Apell*) to check the number of inmates, and forced labour for everyone except the very sick, the very old and the very young. At mealtimes, prisoners formed a long, weary queue for a bowl of watery soup and some hard bread. In the French transit camp Rivesaltes, children were starving. Those who could still walk had to line up for their poor rations. Children, huddled in filthy grey blankets, lined up on the rocky ground with their hands outstretched for scraps of food.

There was no privacy in the transit camps. Toilet and wash facilities were few and filthy. At night, people slept on wooden bunks without blankets or mattresses in barracks that were freezing and often without electricity. Under such conditions, most prisoners soon became ill with exhaustion, hunger or disease. Family life was almost impossible, but children and their parents did their best to stay together and provide support for each other. In some transit camps, there were very basic schools for those children left behind in the barracks while their parents went to work. There were no textbooks and few writing materials. Lessons were given mostly by speech alone, and the children had to listen and remember what they had learned. Classes never stayed the same from one week to the next because most of the teachers and their pupils eventually ended up being deported.

In France, rumours of what was happening to the Jews led the humanitarian organization Oeuvre Secours aux Enfants (OSE) to try to convince the authorities to release some of the children from the transit camps. In the summer of 1942, a number of children *were* handed over to OSE workers. The moment of separation from their parents was very hard. Although parents knew and were glad that their children were being saved, they could hardly bear to let their sons and daughters go. The scenes of departure were heart-rending. Very young children had no idea why they were being separated from their parents and, as they were lined up for the buses that would take them out of the camp, screamed to be allowed to return to them. The older children, who understood something of the anguish their parents felt, tried to be brave and control their own pain until their faces were rigid with the effort of holding back their tears. As the buses drove off, weeping mothers clung to the doors until their arms gave way and they sank to the ground.

In July 1942, 13,000 Jews were captured in Paris, among them 4,000 children. The children were sent, without their parents, to Drancy transit camp in a suburb of Paris. Within two weeks, the children had been deported. An eyewitness recalled watching as the children were woken at five o'clock in the morning and made to dress in the half-light. It was cold in the yard where they were told to wait. The smallest among them howled to go back to their bunks, however uncomfortable they had been. The gendarmes picked up those who had refused to get out of bed and dress, and dragged them down to the yard to wait as their names were called out. Confused with sleep and distress, many of the children did not answer or else responded to the wrong name. The older children tried to comfort them as best they could. In the end, none of the children survived the war.

In 1944, a group of Jewish children arrived in Drancy from an orphanage in the village of Izieu. Teacher Miron Zlatin had taken forty-four Jewish children into the orphanage where he worked and had told no one, other than his staff, that the children were Jewish and were not actually orphans. The youngest child was four, the eldest was seventeen. They were well cared for by the staff and formed close friendships with the other children. One of the hidden children, eleven-year-old Liliane Gerenstein, who was staying at the orphanage with her little brother, wrote a letter to God, which has survived:

God? It is thanks to You that I had a beautiful life before, that I was spoiled, that I had lovely things other people do not have. God? After that I ask You one thing only: make my parents come back. My poor parents, protect them (even more than You protect me) so that I can see them again as soon as possible. Make them come back again. I had such a good mother and a good father. I have such faith in You and I thank You in advance.[102]

Along with all the other Jewish children, Liliane and her brother were caught by the Nazis in April 1944, when SS soldiers raided the orphanage, looking for hidden children. They were sent first to Drancy, then to Auschwitz. Miron Zlatin and two of the children ended up in another camp where they were murdered. In Auschwitz, teacher Léa Feldblum begged the Nazis to let the children go; she told the soldiers on the platform in the camp that the children were from an orphanage, hoping this might change their minds. The SS sent her alone into the camp, then marched the other five teachers and all the children to the gas chambers. Léa Feldblum survived the war.

In Czechoslovakia, the ghetto Theresienstadt served as

a transit camp for Auschwitz. When the Red Cross wanted to visit Theresienstadt to see how the inmates were being treated, the Nazis told them that it was a town given to the Jews by Hitler, mainly inhabited by families of men who had fought for Germany during the First World War. In fact, it was no different from any of the other ghettos, apart from its active artistic community. Children put on musicals, plays, created their own newspaper, wrote stories and painted. The best-known artist to have emerged from Theresienstadt is probably Helga Weissovà-Hoskovà, who arrived in the camp after being taken, at the age of twelve, from her home town of Prague in December 1941. She kept a diary of ghetto life in a series of beautiful paintings. Together with her mother, Helga survived Theresienstadt, Auschwitz and Mathausen, and today she is a successful artist.

Jewish painter Friedl Dicker-Brandeis was also imprisoned in Theresienstadt, where she encouraged children to express their emotions through art. She brought her crayons, paper and paints with her into the ghetto and taught children about colour and creativity. Ela Weissberger was one of those whom Friedl Dicker-Brandeis taught. She remembers: 'Before Brandeis, we were all just sitting there waiting for the next horrible thing to happen. Can you imagine being in a Nazi camp with nothing to do? Brandeis let a lot of light in where there was darkness.'[103] Another girl, twelve-year-old Alice Guttmanova, drew a picture of the deportation train with crayons shortly before being sent to Auschwitz where she was gassed in 1943. Friedl Dicker-Brandeis kept all the artwork in two suitcases. When she heard that she, too, was going to be deported to Auschwitz in October 1944, she buried the suitcases behind a brick wall, hoping that someone would find them after the war. She did not survive, but when the war ended and building work began in the city, workers found the suitcases. The artworks were recently exhibited in the USA, where they were seen by thousands of people.

Of 15,000 children imprisoned in Theresienstadt, only 1,100 survived the war.

4 August 1944 was a warm, still summer's day in Amsterdam. By mid-morning, everyone in the Secret Annexe was in their usual place, reading or studying quietly. In the offices below, Miep, Bep, Kugler and Kleiman were busy with routine tasks, and on the ground floor, the warehousemen were mixing and packing spices. At about 10.30 a.m., a car pulled up in front of the building. Several men got out. One of them asked the warehouseman standing at the door a question. He pointed upstairs, and the men went inside.

In the front office, Miep, Bep and Kleiman all looked up as the door opened, having heard footsteps on the stairs. A man stood in front of them, not in uniform, but holding a gun. 'Don't move', he said. 'Just sit there quietly and don't move.' He went through to the next office, leaving the three of them sitting motionless, in utter shock. Miep suddenly said, 'Bep, we've had it.'

In the office next door, Kugler heard footsteps in the corridor and then his door, too, opened. He started at the sight of the men before him. Several Dutch Nazis stood in the doorway, all dressed in ordinary clothes, apart from their leader, Karl Josef Silberbauer, who wore the uniform of the Gestapo. He asked Kugler who was in charge of the offices.

'I am,' Kugler replied.

One of the other men stepped forward. 'We know everything,' he said. 'You're hiding Jews and they're in this building. Take us to them.'

Kugler felt the blood rush to his face. He knew it was over. He got up and led the way upstairs.

In the front office, Miep searched her bag for the illegal ration cards needed to feed eight people in hiding. She held them in her lap as she dipped into her bag again, taking out money and Jan's lunch. When her husband arrived, a short while later, the Gestapo were still in the building. Miep was able to stop him at the office door. She handed him his lunch, then the money and ration cards for safekeeping, whispering urgently, 'It's wrong here.' He understood and left the building.

Upstairs, Kugler and the Nazis had reached the corridor where the bookcase hid the entrance to the Secret Annexe. Kugler pretended that there was nothing else to see, but the Nazis shook the bookcase until they found the hook holding it against the wall. They lifted it from its latch, and the door to the Secret Annexe was revealed. Silberbauer drew his gun. He pushed Kugler in front of him, the pistol pressing against his spine, and softly gave the order: 'In.'

Kugler walked slowly along the corridor to the left of the staircase. It was unpleasantly humid, as it always was during the summer months. In the Franks' sitting room, Anne's mother was standing alone, beside the table. She looked anxious and confused by Kugler's unexpected appearance. With a great effort, Kugler said, 'The Gestapo are here.'

Downstairs, one of the Dutch Nazis strode into the office where Bep, Miep and Kleiman were still waiting. He told Kleiman to accompany him to Kugler's office. After ten minutes, Kleiman reappeared alone, having been ordered to hand the keys of the building over to Miep. He gave Bep his wallet and told her to take it to a friend, who had a chemist's shop nearby. 'Tell him to pass it on to my wife,' Kleiman said, hoping that at least one of them would escape. Bep ran out of the building, unseen. Before returning to the back office, Kleiman pressed the keys into Miep's palm and whispered, 'See that you stay out of this, Miep. You can't save us, but make the best of a bad thing here.'

Miep nodded, speechless.

Upstairs in the annexe, the Nazis now entered the other secret rooms, rounding everyone up. Mr Frank and Peter were the last to know they had been discovered; they were studying English in Peter's room when they heard someone racing up the stairs. Mr Frank jumped to his feet, astonished. The door flew open and a man pointed a pistol straight at them: 'Raise your hands.' Neither of them said anything: the shock was too great. They followed the man into the van Pelses' room, where Mr and Mrs van Pels and Fritz Pfeffer were standing with their hands above their heads. Another Nazi ordered them downstairs to the first floor of the annexe.

Anne stood silently with her mother and sister in the middle of their sitting room, her hands raised. Margot wept softly.

Kugler was there too. The sun glittered through the thick curtains. Silberbauer turned to Anne's father and asked, 'Where are your valuables?'

Mr Frank pointed to a small cupboard. Silberbauer lifted out a small cashbox containing a few pieces of jewellery and some money. He glanced around and his gaze fell on Mr Frank's briefcase. He picked it up and shook it open. Notebooks, loose papers and a check-covered autograph album fell out: Anne's diary. Anne said nothing. Silberbauer emptied the cashbox into the briefcase, along with a few other objects. 'Have you any weapons?' he asked, snapping the briefcase shut.

They all shook their heads. 'Good,' Silberbauer said. 'Now get ready. I want everyone back here in five minutes.'

It did not take long for them to pack the small 'emergency' bags which they had always intended to use if a bomb fell near the annexe and they needed to escape in a hurry. While everyone was doing that, Silberbauer paced up and down the room. 'How long have you been here?' he asked Anne's father.

When Mr Frank told him it was just over two years, Silberbauer looked amazed. 'Two years?' he said. 'I don't believe you.'

Anne's father showed him some pencil marks on one wall, along with letters and dates and said, 'That's where we've measured the height of my younger daughter while we've been here.'

Silberbauer was further surprised when Mr Frank told him he had been a lieutenant in the German army during the First World War. From that moment, his manner changed slightly. He told everyone they could take their time packing their things, and he told his men to allow them some space to do this. Later, Mr Frank recalled, 'Anne walked back and forth, and did not even glance at her diary. Perhaps she had a premonition that all was lost now.'[104]

When they had all gathered their belongings, Silberbauer ordered them along the corridor to the swinging bookcase. When they were all in the hallway, one of the Nazis locked the door and shoved the bookcase back into place.

Alone in her office, Miep heard them coming down the wooden staircase 'like beaten dogs'.[105]

They gathered in the private office and stood there silently. Silberbauer fired questions, first at Kugler, then at Kleiman. Their answer was always: 'I have nothing to say.'

'All right,' Silberbauer snapped, his colour rising. 'Then you'll come along too.'

A group of curious onlookers had gathered near the waiting police van in front of the warehouse. Among them was Jan Gies with Kleiman's brother, and the warehouse clerks. The ten prisoners – the Franks, the van Pelses, Pfeffer and Kleiman and Kugler – climbed into the van. The bells of the Westerkerk rang out. Then the doors slammed shut and darkness fell around them.

Following their arrest, the Franks, the van Pelses, Pfeffer, Kugler and Kleiman were taken to Gestapo headquarters in south Amsterdam. In the courtyard a black flag bearing the emblem of the SS flew from a tall white pole. The offices were in a large, red-brick former school. The ten prisoners were led into this building and locked in a room with several other prisoners. They seemed numbed. Anne, Margot and Peter occasionally whispered to each other. Mr Frank turned to

Kleiman and said in a low voice, 'You can't imagine how I feel. To think that you are sitting here among us, that we are to blame –'

'Don't give it another thought,' said Kleiman. 'It was up to me and I wouldn't have done it any differently.'

After a while, Kugler and Kleiman were taken to another cell. Apart from Otto Frank, they never saw their friends again.

The Franks, the van Pelses and Pfeffer were taken into Silberbauer's office for questioning. Mr Frank was asked if he knew where any other Jews were hiding. He replied that he did not; having been in hiding himself for two years, he had lost touch with everyone. Silberbauer believed him. The prisoners returned to their cells for the night, but the following day they were transferred to the Weteringschans jail in the centre of Amsterdam. It was a huge, ugly building with two wings extending out from a centre block, overlooking a filthy stretch of canal. Metal bars were at the windows. The Franks, the van Pelses and Pfeffer remained there for two days.

On 8 August, four days after their arrest, the Franks and their friends were taken to Amsterdam's Centraal Station. The train that arrived to take them out of the city looked like an ordinary one, but as soon as the passengers climbed aboard, the doors were locked and bolted behind them. Despite this, they were hopeful for the future, since by now it was clear that the Germans were losing the war. Anne stayed by the window throughout the journey, spellbound by the countryside. For a short while, it was almost like freedom, but by late afternoon the train had reached its destination: Kamp Westerbork.

*　　*　　*

Westerbork was in Drenthe, eighty miles north of Amsterdam, and in a very lonely spot. Before the war it was set up by the Dutch government as a refugee camp for German Jews. When war broke out, the refugees were evacuated so that the Germans could redesign the camp. The refugees returned when it was completed, now as a transit camp. A high barbed-wire fence surrounded 107 wooden barracks, each containing three-tier bunks, enough to house 300 people. Work began at five o'clock in the morning for the inmates, who had to take apart old aeroplane batteries while the guards watched over them. The commandant of Westerbork, Alfred Gemmeker, lived in a house on the edge of the camp and ran a small chicken farm.

Irene Butter-Hasenberg was twelve years old when she arrived in Westerbork. Her first impression was how dark it was that night; soon she was in a line, waiting to be checked for head lice, then undressing with hundreds of other strangers as doctors examined everyone. Men and women were separated and those who were found to have lice had their heads shaved. Irene did not have lice, but it instilled in her a fear that she would catch them and lose her hair. She looked around her at the newly bald inmates. She didn't recognize any of them without their hair and it terrified her. Despite her experiences in the camps, Irene survived the war.

Like Irene, and Anne Frank, Eva Geiringer was sent to the camp. Her feelings upon arrival were different from those of Irene: 'We hadn't been especially afraid of going to Westerbork. It wasn't a concentration camp and we thought we might stay there until the liberation. I was very happy to be with my father and brother again . . . We had begun to be really hopeful again. We never thought that we wouldn't survive.'[106] But each week a list was made of those who would be deported from Westerbork, either to Sobibor or to Auschwitz. To their horror, one evening Eva and her family heard their names read out: 'We tried everything we could to change things, but it was no good. The people who compiled the list were mainly Jews, I think, and they did what they could to protect their friends and relatives. But for the rest, well, we just had to go. Everyone packed what they had, though later they took it all from us.'[107]

When the Franks, the van Pelses and Pfeffer arrived at Westerbork on the afternoon of 8 August, they went through the usual routine for new arrivals. They were sent first to the registration desks in the main square. Ration cards were handed over, then personal information was entered on forms and cards. The woman who took down the Franks' details was a Jewish prisoner, Vera Cohn. She recalled:

Mr Frank was a pleasant-looking man, courteous and cultured. He stood before me tall and straight. He answered my routine questions quietly. Anne was by his side. Her face, by certain standards, was not a pretty one, but her eyes – bright, young, eager eyes – made you look at her again. She was fifteen then . . . none of the Franks showed any signs of despair over their plight . . . Their composure, as they grouped around my typing desk in the receiving room, was one of quiet dignity.[108]

*   *   *

Before being led to their barracks, all newcomers were asked if they had any valuables with them, and they were thoroughly searched. Because they had been in hiding, the Franks and their friends were 'convict Jews', which meant that they were held in the punishment compound, Barrack 67. Their freedom was limited, even by the standards of the camp. Instead of keeping their own clothes they were given blue overalls with red shoulder-patches, and wooden clogs. Men had their heads shaved and women had their hair cropped. They were not allowed any soap and they received less food than the other prisoners, even though their work was harder.

On their first day in the camp, the Franks met Mr and Mrs de Winter and their daughter Judy, who was the same age as Anne. The de Winters had been in hiding for over a year when a spy betrayed them to the Gestapo. They became close to the Franks in Westerbork. Each day they all attended roll-call before work began at five o'clock in the morning. Children were sent to the cable workshop and adults to the industrial department, where they spent the day at long tables, taking apart old aeroplane batteries. They could talk to each other, but guards stood over them while they worked, yelling at them to speed up. Lunch was stale bread and watery soup. Working alongside the Franks were two sisters, Janny and Lientje Brilleslijper. Lientje recalled, 'The two girls, Margot and Anne, were very attached to their mother. Anne wrote in her diary that her mother didn't understand her, but I think that was just an adolescent mood. She clung to her mother in the camp.'[109]

Also in the punishment block was Rachel van Amerongen-Frankfoorder. She had worked for the Resistance before being caught and sent to Westerbork. Rachel worked for Westerbork's internal service, and Mr Frank asked her if she could find another job for Anne. Rachel realized that Anne was the apple of her father's eye and that he was keen to do anything that might help make life in the camp a little easier for her. Anne said, 'I can do everything – I'm very handy,' but there was nothing that Rachel could offer her.

Mrs de Winter also noticed the closeness between Mr Frank and his younger daughter. She liked Mr Frank, whose quiet manner was reassuring to everyone around him. When Anne fell sick, her father came over from the men's barracks to comfort her and he stood beside her bed for hours, telling her stories. When Anne recovered, she copied her father's example; when a young boy named David became ill, she visited him and talked to him for hours. David was from an Orthodox Jewish family and he and Anne talked about God.

In his memoir, Mr Frank recalled:

At the camp we had to work, although we had the evenings off and we could be together. It was a particular relief for the children to no longer be locked away and to be able to talk with other people. We, the older ones, however, feared the danger of being transported to the rumoured death camps of Poland . . .[110]

At the beginning of September, the man in charge of Westerbork, Alfred Gemmeker, called the section leaders to his office and told them to put together a new list for deportation. The train was due to leave on the morning of 3 September 1944. The night before, one of the section leaders and an official entered the punishment barracks to read out the names on the list: '... and Hermann, Auguste and Peter van Pels, Fritz Pfeffer, Otto, Edith, Margot and Anne Frank ...'

What was it like on board the deportation train? Rabbi Hugo Gryn was deported from Hungary in 1944 at the age of thirteen. He recalled later the unbearable heat inside the train carriage and the toilet bucket that stank to high heaven. Although there was food, there was no water except a bit in a barrel that was warm and full of dirt. Soon they were travelling through a landscape none of the passengers recognized and past stations whose names they could not read. But they knew that they were in Poland. Everyone was exhausted, and no one spoke. The train raced on and the young Hugo felt as though he were going slowly mad: 'The heat, the thirst, the dirt – everything seemed to conspire against me.'

Sherry Weiss-Rosenfeld was fifteen years old when she was sent to Auschwitz with her aunt and uncle in May 1944. The journey was an unimaginable nightmare, with people packed into the train compartments until it was impossible to turn around or have even the smallest space for oneself. One night there was a storm and the rain poured in through the wooden slats, bringing relief to everyone, for there was no water on board for them to drink.

During the night before Anne Frank and her family were due to depart Westerbork transit camp, all those whose names had been read out packed the few belongings they still had and exchanged addresses where they could meet after the war, in the event of separation. Mrs de Winter gave her daughter, Judy, the address of her aunt in Zutphen, and the Franks decided to meet in Switzerland.

As the sun rose on 3 September, the main street of Westerbork camp was being closed off. The train itself had already arrived, a long chain of trucks that had rolled quietly into the camp during the night. On the platform stood Alfred Gemmeker with his dog at his side. Guards strolled about, relaxed and smiling. At seven o'clock that morning, men, women and children began filing out of the barracks. Each passenger carried a rucksack and a rolled-up blanket. They were instructed to walk forward in groups of three.

The sick and disabled were guided through on stretchers and carts. It was a high step up from the platform to the train, and a long wait until the carriages were filled. As doors closed, people put their hands through the gaps in the wooden slats. There were no windows in the train; these were the dreaded cattle trucks: dark, airless and unbearably claustrophobic.

At eleven o'clock, the whistle blew. The guards still standing on the platform could read the inscription on the back of the train as it pulled away: 'Westerbork–Auschwitz: Auschwitz–Westerbork. Do not uncouple the carriages, the entire train must return to Westerbork intact.' The ninety-third transport from Westerbork contained 1,019 people (498 women, 442 men and 79 children).

It was the very last train to leave Holland for Auschwitz.

Anne and her family and the friends they had made in

Westerbork sat together on their rucksacks, pressing themselves against the walls. They shared their carriage with the desperately sick. It was cramped – seventy-five people were packed tightly together – and it became cold as they travelled by night. Straw lay on the floor and there was a small bucket filled with drinking water. A larger bucket served as a toilet, and next to it lay a sandbag to soak up any spillage. A small lantern swung from the ceiling. It smelled terrible, and later the stench became worse when people had to use the toilet bucket and the weak began to die.

Hours passed, and they knew they were in Germany. Whenever the train stopped, a guard would open a door and throw in a bucket of beetroot and a few pieces of bread. Sometimes they stopped for hours and a guard would shout for them to hand over any valuables they had left.

Anne, Margot, Peter and Judy sat together, talking quietly and occasionally climbing up on the bars to peep out of a long hole in the wooden slats. A young man who was keeping watch stepped aside for them; he had been trying to work out whether they really were making for Poland, as the rumours had said.

At night it was impossible to sleep. The jarring of the cattle trucks, the smell and the fear kept them all awake. Tempers frayed and people argued, shouted and sobbed. Everyone was exhausted. In his memoir, Mr Frank recalled the journey in just two sentences: 'The awful transportation – three days locked in a cattle truck – was the last time I saw my family. Each of us tried to be as courageous as possible and not to let our heads drop.'[111]

On the night of the third day, the train began to slow down.

The passengers got to their feet, steeling themselves. A murmur of voices praying filled the cattle cars. The train turned sharply in the direction of a long, low building with an arched entrance and a high, pointed roof. Searchlight beams swept across marshland, and in the distance dogs barked fiercely.

The train stopped. Rifle butts pounded on the doors and German voices began to shout: 'Jews, out, quickly, OUT!'

9

'Who Has Inflicted This Upon Us?'

About 216,000 Jewish children were sent to Auschwitz. Just under 7,000 were allowed into the camp to work; the rest were sent to the gas chambers. When Auschwitz was liberated in January 1945, only 451 Jews under the age of sixteen were still alive.

In theory, children under the age of fifteen did not exist in Auschwitz. Because they were too weak to withstand the punishing work in the camp, they were usually sent to the gas chambers as soon as they arrived, along with their mothers. A few children survived the selection on the ramp, when newcomers were separated into two groups: those who would live and those who would die. Some of the children who were allowed into Auschwitz were used as guinea pigs in scientific experiments, others were judged strong enough to work. The only children certain to survive the first selection for the gas chambers were twins. Josef Mengele, the SS doctor in charge of the selections, was fascinated by twins and was keen to use them in his experiments. Some were no more than five years old. But Mengele's experiments were so cruel that hardly any of the 3,000 twins admitted to Auschwitz survived.

On 5 September 1944, when the doors of the Westerbork train were wrenched apart, the first thing Anne Frank and her family saw were glaring searchlights fixed on the train and, outside on the platform, men running back and forth. The men were *kapos*, and they reached into the carriages to pull those nearest to them down on to the uneven ground. Behind the *kapos*, SS officers greeted the Nazi guards who had accompanied the train from Holland.

The *kapos* yelled at the newcomers to hurry. There were shouts and screams of anguish as relatives disappeared from view. The *kapos* rushed through, dragging luggage from the train and stacking it at the back of the platform. The bodies of those who had died during the journey were left beside the suitcases. Above the hissing steam of the cooling train, a loudspeaker bellowed: 'Women to the left! Men to the right!' Anne watched her father, Hermann van Pels, Peter van Pels and Fritz Pfeffer being herded away by the SS along with all the other male passengers. It was the last time Anne ever saw her beloved father.

The guards stepped forward, shoving the women into columns of five and then again into two rows. The selection to decide who would live and who would die began. Anne stood with her mother and Margot and Mrs van Pels on the platform, watching as Mengele moved among the crowd. His silver hair gleamed in the light. With a flick of his wrist, he sent Anne, Mrs Frank, Margot and Mrs van Pels to join the queue of those who would live.

The loudspeaker roared again: 'It's an hour's march to the women's camp. For children and the sick we've provided lorries at the end of the platform. Hurry!' The trucks were painted with red crosses, and people ran towards them, hanging on desperately as the engines started. Within minutes, they had disappeared. None of them was ever seen again.

Anne's group was forced to march quickly. They saw the blue gleam of the electrified fences that ran the length of the camp and silhouetted figures standing motionless in the watchtowers. This was Birkenau, the women's camp in Auschwitz, 'the greatest death-factory of all'. There was no longer any doubt about where they were.

The women were led into a narrow building and forced to undress. They stood under the showers while their clothes were taken away. They were then shaved of all their hair. Finally, they were given the camp uniform: shoes and a grey, sack-like dress, some with crosses on the back marking them out as new arrivals. Wearing their sacks, they went across to a row of desks, where they gave their personal details and had their forearms tattooed with their prisoner number. All newcomers were then assigned to their barracks. Anne, Margot, Mrs Frank, Mrs de Winter and her daughter, Judy, were all placed in Block 29 (Mrs van Pels had become separated from them in the panic). It was a block identical to all the others: a long, low room in semi-permanent darkness, with rows of wooden bunks in tiers of three, filled with straw or with straw mattresses. The floor swam with urine and excrement.

Each day of Anne's existence in Auschwitz followed the

same punishing routine: rising at 3.30 a.m., then rushing to the latrine block and back for 'breakfast'. Every woman had to hang on to the bowl she had been given for her food; the bowls could not be replaced if they were lost, except through 'organizing' – camp slang for stealing or bartering. Anne got hold of a pair of men's long johns from another woman by 'organizing' them. Until then, like the other inmates, she had worn nothing but a grey sack, under which she was naked.

After breakfast came roll-call. Anne and the other women had to stand in rows of five in the square while block-leaders counted them. Roll-call in the morning usually lasted forty-five minutes. Evening roll-call could last from an hour to five hours. The women were forced to stand in sun, rain, hail or snow for as long as the roll-call leader chose and while punishments were carried out. Ronnie Goldstein-van Cleef, who had been in Westerbork with the Franks, often stood beside Anne during roll-call. They always shared a mug of 'coffee', although the liquid didn't taste much like real coffee. Margot stood nearby, either next to Anne or in front of her, depending on how the rows of five worked out.

The march to work from Anne's block took half an hour. The work itself consisted of digging an area of grass, which they tossed on top of a pile. It was completely pointless, but the *kapos* ran among them constantly, screaming, 'Faster! Faster!' and beating those who couldn't work quickly enough. At 12.30 p.m., huge vats of soup were carried into the field. Each woman held out her bowl and received one ladle's worth of greasy fluid. For half an hour they sat in groups of five, drinking from their bowls, and then they returned to work. At 6 p.m., they were given their evening meal: a slice of bread and a tiny piece of margarine. The block-leader's assistant distributed the bread. Anne was made an assistant. Mrs de Winter remembered: 'Anne was the youngest in her group, but nevertheless she was the leader of it. She also distributed the bread in the barracks, and she did it so well and so fairly that there was none of the usual grumbling.'[112] At 9 p.m., the whistles blew and they were allowed into the barracks.

Although the prisoners had survived the selection on the platform when they arrived, they were under constant threat of being sent to the gas chambers. There were regular selections in all the barracks, and no one knew when it might be their turn. Four gas chambers in the camp worked day and night, and during the time of Anne's imprisonment in Auschwitz, as many as 24,000 people were gassed in a single day. Not surprisingly, the prisoners needed each other for support, and they tried to remain in groups of family and friends for as long as possible. Anne, her mother and sister and Mrs de Winter and Judy de Winter stayed with three women they had known in Westerbork: Bloem Evers-Emden, Lenie de Jong-van Naarden and Ronnie Goldstein-van Cleef. Bloem recalls that Mrs Frank and her two daughters were always together and gave each other a great deal of support. Mrs Frank's only thought was for her daughters. She stayed with them constantly and tried her hardest to find them something to eat.

On 27 October, there was a selection in Anne's block. This time it wasn't for the gas chambers but for work in a Czechoslovakian munitions factory, making weapons for the Nazi war effort. Everyone desperately wanted to be chosen, knowing that they would have a far greater chance of survival outside Auschwitz. Judy de Winter and Bloem Evers-Emden were among those taken. Anne, Margot and their mother remained in Auschwitz. They were rejected because Anne had scabies, a disease set off by lice getting under the skin and causing painful red and black sores that itch intensely. Mrs Frank and Margot wouldn't leave Anne alone in the camp, even though this meant putting their own lives at greater risk. Bloem spoke to Mrs Frank, who was with Margot. Anne was in the scabies barracks. Mrs Frank said, 'We are, of course, staying with her.' Margot nodded. Bloem understood how they felt, that they were unable to abandon Anne for their own sakes. It was the last time she saw them.

Soon after Anne was put in the scabies barracks, Margot joined her there voluntarily. Lenie de Jong-van Naarden remembers that Mrs Frank was in complete despair about her daughters. She refused to eat the tiny piece of bread she was given as her ration each day. Instead, she asked Lenie to dig a hole under the wooden wall of the scabies barracks, where the ground was quite soft. Mrs Frank stood beside her all the time, asking, 'Is it working?' Lenie told her that it was. When the hole was big enough, they were able to speak to Margot and Anne, and to pass the bread through to them. Inevitably, Margot also caught scabies. Ronnie Goldstein-van Cleef, who was in the barracks with them and another girl named Frieda Brommet, remembered how Frieda's mother and Mrs Frank searched the entire camp, looking for scraps of food to give to the sick girls.

On one occasion, Ronnie found a platinum watch inside her

mattress where a previous prisoner had hidden it. She slipped it through the hole under the barracks to Mrs Frank and Mrs Brommet, who exchanged it for a whole loaf of bread, a piece of cheese and a piece of sausage. Margot and Anne needed all the food they could get because their health was failing rapidly. Ronnie remembers that the two girls hardly spoke to anyone. They livened up slightly when the food arrived, but only to share it and eat. Ronnie sometimes sang for them, trying to keep their spirits up. She was shocked by their appearance; they looked terrible, covered in spots and sores from the scabies. They put some ointment on their wounds, but it didn't help.

On 30 October 1944, there was another selection in the women's camp at Auschwitz-Birkenau. Only sixty miles away, the Russians were advancing. The cry of 'Block closed!' went up at evening roll-call. Anne and Margot and their mother, together with the friends they had made in Westerbork, were among those marched to the large square and forced to undress. They remained there, naked, for two days. Their friend Lientje Brilleslijper recalled: 'We stood there. Standing, standing, then a few steps and then standing again, with only a small piece of hard bread for nourishment. Then we were whipped into a big hall where it was at least warm. Here the selection took place.'[113]

Josef Mengele stood impatiently beside the blue gleam of the spotlights. Lientje recalled, 'He made us step on a scale and then waved his hand right or left to indicate life or death. Just a casual wave – to the gas chamber.'[114] Anne stood with her mother and sister and Mrs de Winter in the queue. It took a long time until they reached the front of the line. Realizing that Mengele was picking out the old and the sick, the women took several years off their actual age and lied about their health. Mrs de Winter called out, 'I am twenty-nine and I have never had dysentery yet.'[115] But Mengele sent her to join the old and the sick – those who would be gassed. Then it was Mrs Frank's turn, and he sent her, too, to join the same group.

'Next!' Mengele shouted.

Anne and Margot walked forward. They were still in a pitiful condition from the scabies, but they were both young. Mrs de Winter and Mrs Frank waited in terror, hoping desperately that they would not join their group on the right. The women on the left did not know what their fate would be, but at least they would not be sent to the gas chambers.

Anne said something to encourage Margot, who walked naked and shaven-headed into the light. They stood together for a moment, and Anne looked over at her mother. She stood very still and straight, her face expressionless.

'To the left!' Mengele shouted, and Anne and Margot walked on.

At that moment of separation from her daughters, Mrs Frank let out an anguished scream: 'The children! O God, the children . . . !'

Mrs Frank never saw her daughters again. Although she and Mrs de Winter were rescued from the gas chambers by a prisoner who managed to drag them away from the waiting queue, Mrs Frank never recovered from losing her children. Without them, and separated from her husband, she lost the will to live.

Edith Frank died of hunger and distress in Auschwitz on 6 January 1945.

The war was gradually coming to an end. Germany was losing ground on all fronts and German cities were being heavily bombed by the Allies, which killed thousands. In Auschwitz, the SS began to destroy all evidence of their crimes. Gassings stopped in November 1944 and the gas chambers were destroyed. The cremating pits, containing mounds of human ash, were raked over and planted with grass seed. Some of the Kanada warehouses – containing the clothes and possessions of prisoners – were set on fire and thousands of documents were burned. In mid January 1945, the SS abandoned Auschwitz. The Russians were closing in, and the fleeing SS decided to evacuate all prisoners able to walk.

Across Europe, survivors of ghettos, deportations, slave labour and concentration camps were herded through the countryside on 'death marches' away from the liberators. Most had to walk in freezing temperatures; others were put on open trucks. Prisoners, starved and beaten by the German guards accompanying them, were sometimes mistaken for German military by Russian soldiers, who would open fire on them. Most of the prisoners died of exhaustion; those who couldn't keep up were shot and their bodies left where they had died.

The death marches were a cheap way of getting prisoners away from the Allied liberators and into the concentration camps of Germany, where they were put to work or left to die without food, water or medical attention. For many of the prisoners, their destination was Bergen-Belsen. This camp, in northern Germany, had been set up as a prisoner-of-war camp for French and Belgian soldiers, but since 1943, Jews had been sent there and the camp was taken over by the SS. They began bringing in sick prisoners from other camps, although there was no medication, sanitation or care for them, and almost no food. In December, a new commandant, Josef Kramer, arrived from Auschwitz with his cruellest staff. He put *kapos* in charge of the camp and deliberately starved prisoners.

By early 1945, the camp was swollen with death march survivors. There was even less food and water than before and desperate prisoners ate grass to fill their empty stomachs. And then a typhus epidemic broke out.

Anne and Margot left Auschwitz in a transport of 634 women at the beginning of November 1944, after the selection. They had been given old clothing, odd shoes, a blanket, a quarter of a loaf of bread, 150 grams of sausage and a little margarine for their journey. No one knew where they were going, but the journey in the cattle cars was appalling. It was bitterly cold and cramped in the wagons and they received no more food or water. After four days, the train stopped and the SS guards unbolted the doors. The exhausted, frozen women climbed out on to the platform at Celle station. The concentration camp of Bergen-Belsen was a few miles away.

Lientje and Janny Brilleslijper were also on the transport

from Auschwitz. As they wandered around Belsen, they met Margot and Anne again. Lientje recalled:

We had a look around, and heard that there was a tap on a little hill. We hurried there to wash. And as the two of us went up the hill, two thin figures approached, and we fell about one another's necks. The two spoke Dutch. We were four shaven-headed figures, thin and shaking. Anne and Margot had many questions, and we, too, had many questions. We asked about their mother, for we knew that in Auschwitz the men had been separated from the group. Anne began to cry bitterly, and Margot said quite softly, 'Selected.'[116]

The four girls sat together on the hill, watching the line of exhausted prisoners from Celle station approach. Lientje looked at Anne and Margot as they huddled beneath their blankets:

The two were inseparable, like my sister and I. They looked like two frozen birds, it was painful to look at them. After we had washed, naked in the open air, we were speedily dressed, for we had nothing except a dress and a thin blanket, a blanket which one treasured like a costly possession. Then we crept together in one of the tents.[117]

At first Anne and Margot argued over whether to enter the tents, but they decided it would be better than staying outside. Janny Brilleslijper recalled that they waited until the last moment and then went into the tent. It was boiling hot inside because so many people were herded in there together. It stank terribly, and the rain lashed down on the roof, making holes in the tent. They slept on thin layers of straw, squeezed together with 200 others. There was no lighting and no toilets.

On the evening of 7 November, a wild storm broke out over the heath. The gale ripped up the tents and threw them to the ground. Women screamed and cowered as tent poles crashed down around them. They crouched in the open air in the pouring rain, until a group of SS guards arrived and drove them into the kitchen tent, hitting them as they ran.

The following day, still shivering with cold, they were moved on again. 'We were put in an old barn filled with rags and old shoes,' Lientje remembered. 'Anne asked, "Why do they want us to become animals?"'[118]

For a few days, the Brilleslijper sisters became separated from Margot and Anne. Eventually, they ended up in the same barracks, sleeping on wooden bunks in a stone hut, where several thousand people had only one washroom between them. Before long, the camp was like a huge open sewer and those who died were left where they were. More transports kept arriving from other camps, and Belsen became dangerously overcrowded.

Anne and Margot had the bunk below Lientje and Janny in their barracks. Their spirits had not yet been completely broken by the misery surrounding them. 'Anne used to tell stories after we lay down,' Lientje remembered. 'So did Margot. Silly stories and jokes. We all took turns telling them. Mostly they were about food. Once we talked about going to the American Hotel in Amsterdam for dinner and Anne suddenly burst into tears at the thought that we would never get back.'[119]

The girls were put to work in the shoe-shed, a former stables where old shoes from Germany lay in huge piles. The shoes had to be unstitched by hand, the leather soles ripped away, and the usable pieces put to one side. The work was difficult and painful, made worse by the constant beatings they received from the SS. Lientje and Anne found it impossible, as Lientje recalled:

Our hands began to fester. Several people died of blood poisoning. Anne and I were the first who had to stop working. Margot and my sister stood it for rather longer, but they shared their food with us . . . we got for this a little more watery soup and a piece of bread . . . Anne and I began to 'organize' things, to steal from the kitchen or to beg . . . but we never stole from another prisoner. We only stole from the Nazis.[120]

At the end of November, Mrs van Pels arrived in the camp. Margot and Anne had not seen her since the journey from Westerbork, two months before. She immediately became part of their small group. She was with them when they celebrated Christmas and Hannukah in the camp, having gathered all the scraps of food they could find. Crouched under the sloping roof of their barracks, the women sang their favourite songs. Lientje remembered:

Jewish songs . . . and [we] wept. Anne's eyes glittered. She told us stories. We thought they must be old stories which we did not happen to know. But now I know that they were stories she had made up herself. Margot started to tell a story too, but she could not go on and Anne completed it for her. She said that her father knew much better stories and Margot began to cry, asking whether he was still alive. Anne was confident, 'Of course he is alive.'[121]

Whenever a new transport arrived in the camp, Anne always wanted to know whether any of her friends from Amsterdam were among them. Lientje remembered:

We were taken to another part of the camp. A group of older women and children were also brought there. Anne came excitedly to us, 'Let's go there, maybe there are friends among them, they are said to be all Dutch.' She wanted to go over immediately. At this moment, I believe, she was the Anne which we know from the diary, mercurial and full of life; at other times I only saw her serious and sad. There were some boys and girls whom Anne knew . . . She asked after other friends and learned that Lies, a good friend of hers, was quite near, and she could speak to her in the evening if she was careful.[122]

After hearing that Lies was in the camp, Anne rushed to the barbed-wire fence, where her friend was waiting. The two girls cried when they saw each other. Lies explained that her mother had died and her father was seriously ill. She was in the camp with her little sister, whom Anne used to babysit in Amsterdam. In contrast to what she had said at Christmas, Anne now told Lies that she believed her father had been killed in Auschwitz. When she said that she had nothing to eat, Lies – who still received Red Cross parcels in her part of the camp – brought her food. After one more meeting, the two of them lost contact. Lies's father died, and Lies herself became sick.

In another barracks nearby was a group of Dutch children whom Anne, Margot, Lientje and Janny visited regularly. They sang to them and told them stories to keep their spirits up. Janny and Lientje also became nurses in a new barracks filled with dying Dutch women and children. The girls asked Margot and Anne whether they would like to help, but neither was strong enough to care for anyone else. The Brilleslijpers stole from the Nazi pharmacy and handed out the medicines to those who needed it most. They lost touch with Anne and Margot, who were moved to another barracks. Lientje eventually found out where they were and went to visit them. She remembered:

Margot had an attack of dysentery and could not stand and because of the danger of typhus infection she had to stay in the old block. Anne looked after her as well as she could. We were able to bring them a little food which we had organized. A few days later we heard that they were in the sickbay. We went there and urged them not to stay because if they stayed lying they would perish. But it was at least warm there and there were only two of them in the bunk. Anne said, 'We are together and we have our peace.' Margot scarcely said anything. She had a high fever and smiled contentedly. Her mind was already wandering . . .[123]

Although it was obvious that a German surrender would soon be declared, the Nazis still went on with their 'Final Solution' until the very end. On 20 April 1945, one of the last groups of Jewish children alive in Germany was killed in Hamburg.

The children – ten boys and ten girls – had been sent in November 1944 from Auschwitz to Neuengamme concentration camp for use in medical experiments. They were aged between five and twelve and had come from all over Europe. On 20 April, SS doctor Kurt Heissmeyer and his assistant, Arnold Strippel, decided to kill the children so that the Allied liberators would not find out about their experiments. Heissmeyer sent the children to the old Bullenhuser Damm school in Hamburg; it had been used during the war as a sub-camp. The children were killed in the basement there.

After the war, Heissmeyer returned to his old town of Magdeburg and continued to work as a doctor. Eventually his past caught up with him and in 1966 he was sentenced to life imprisonment. Arnold Strippel was never brought to trial, despite repeated efforts by the parents of the murdered children. He lived the rest of his life unpunished, in a villa in a suburb of Frankfurt.

Today, the room at Bullenhuser Damm where the children died is kept as a memorial to them. Outside is a beautiful garden where anyone who wants to remember the children can plant a rose in their memory.

In one of Belsen's rotting, overcrowded barracks, Margot and Anne lay in agony from typhus. Their bunk was in one of the worst places of all: beside the barrack door, where draughts came stinging through, night and day. Rachel van Amerongen-Frankfoorder, who had not seen either of them since Westerbork, was shocked at the change in them both; they were no longer recognizable, thinner than ever, bald, and with sunken faces. They were very weak, but they still went each day to visit the prisoners who received food from the Red Cross, hoping for something to eat. Sometimes they quarrelled because of their illness, and whenever anyone came in or went out of the barracks, they screamed, 'Close the door! Close the door!' Each day their voices became weaker.

Typhus, caused by infected lice, spread very swiftly in Belsen because there were no medicines to fight it. Those ill with the disease, like Margot and Anne, suffered skin rashes, fever, acute headaches and pain everywhere. When Lientje and her sister visited Margot and Anne again, they knew they did not have long to live: 'Margot had fallen from the bunk and was half-unconscious. Anne was already very feverish. She was very friendly and loving: "Margot will sleep well and when she sleeps I don't need to get up any more."'[124]

Margot was too weak to survive the fall on to the cold stone floor. The shock killed her. With her sister dead, Anne now gave up hope, and the typhus took hold of her small, wasted body. Janny remembered that Anne was very sick but stayed on her feet until Margot died. She approached Janny one day, wearing only a blanket, nothing else. 'I can't stand the fleas and the lice in my clothes,' she told Janny. 'I've thrown everything away. This is all I have.' Janny gave her some clothing and bread. But she saw that Anne had given in to her illness. The death of Margot was more than Anne could bear. She thought that she had nothing left to live for. Her father had actually been liberated from Auschwitz and was on his way back to Amsterdam, asking everyone he met whether they had any news of his daughters, but Anne did not know that.

Just a few days after the death of her sister, Anne died in Belsen, alone.

When Lientje and Janny visited the barracks again, the bunk on which Anne and Margot had lain was empty. They knew immediately that the two girls were dead, and they searched through the pile of corpses until they found them. Lientje remembers: 'Four of us laid the thin bodies on a blanket and carried them to the great open grave. We could do no more.'[125]

On 15 April 1945, only three weeks after the death of Anne Frank, British troops liberated Belsen.

10

'I Want to Go On Living Even After My Death . . .'

On 30 April 1945, Adolf Hitler committed suicide. It was the end of the Nazi reign of terror, the end of the Third Reich. Without their leader to guide them, the German army surrendered on 8 May 1945, and the last concentration camps were liberated.

The reaction of Allied soldiers liberating the concentration camps was one of horror and disbelief. In Bergen-Belsen, British troops made the SS bury some of the 10,000 corpses lying about in the camp, but, to stop typhus from spreading further, huge pits were dug and the bodies pushed in with bulldozers. People who lived nearby and who said they had known nothing about the camp were brought in and marched through the barracks. A British army captain told them: 'What you will see here is such a disgrace to the German people that their name must be eradicated from the list of civilized nations.'

Many children, especially those in the camps, could not believe they were free. Eva Geiringer, who had been imprisoned in Auschwitz with her mother, remembers that on 27 January 1945:*

We heard someone screaming outside. The barrack door was flung open and a woman yelled, 'There's a bear at the gate! A bear at the gate! Come quickly!' Cautiously, we went outside towards the open gate and there, at the entrance, was the 'bear' – a huge being, covered from head to foot in bearskin, with a look of utter amazement on his face. We stood and stared at each other, and then carefully I edged towards him with joy on my face. Our liberator stood at the entrance to the camp, alone and strong. With outstretched arms I ran to him and hugged against him . . . and although our languages were not the same, what I said to him and what he said to me was understood by us both.[126]

Other children had unhappier experiences. A young girl called Cornelia had survived in hiding but knew that her family had been deported to Sobibor. She didn't feel any joy when she was able to leave her hiding place and couldn't understand why people were singing and dancing in the streets. Their joy had little to do with her; she had lost her entire family.

Five-year-old Robert Krell, also in hiding, didn't want

---

* *27 January 1945*: The day on which Auschwitz was liberated is now Holocaust Day, the date on which we officially remember all those who suffered and died in the concentration camps. Not all the concentration camps were liberated at the same time; it depended on where they were in relation to the Allied advance. Mauthausen, for example, was not liberated until the beginning of May.

to go back to his parents, who had survived too. He hadn't seen them in three years and couldn't believe that the strangers standing before him were his mother and father: 'I cried in protest, and they had to prove I was theirs, with photos taken when I was aged about one and a half. Of course, I was actually the luckiest of all children in having my parents alive. Try telling that to a five-year-old with no memory of them, after nearly three years with another family.'[127]

New experiences made others realize that their freedom was not a dream but reality. Arek Hersh from Poland was a prisoner on a crowded train heading towards Theresienstadt when he was liberated. They had reached a railway station called Roudnice and after a few minutes everyone was ordered to get off the train. Arek saw a Czech policeman giving some boys a bit of bread and meat. Suddenly a Ukranian guard stepped forward and turned his rifle to hit the boys with it. The Czech policeman drew his revolver and pointed it at the guard, warning, 'If you touch this child, I will shoot you.' Arek watched in amazement as the guard put down his rifle and walked away: He realized that for the first time in his life he had just witnessed an SS guard taking orders from someone else.

For some, facing the world again was a frightening experience. Sixteen-year-old Benjamin Bender was liberated at Buchenwald on 11 April 1945. He felt weak as he got to his feet and stared around at the other inmates, who were so starved and diseased that they did not grasp the fact that they were free. Benjamin felt no joy in his heart, only 'an aching emptiness'.

A few children immediately felt that they now had a mission in life, having survived against all the odds. Yehuda Bakon, a death march survivor, asked an Allied soldier for a pencil and began feverishly drawing all he could remember: the gas chambers, the undressing rooms and the crematorium, the things he had seen and heard. He had always intended to record everything: 'I asked the *Sonderkommando* men [prisoners who had to work at the gas chambers] to tell me so that if one day I will come out, I will tell the world.'[128]

Of the eight people who had hidden in the secret annexe, Anne's father, Otto Frank, was the only one to survive. He was still in Auschwitz when it was liberated, living in the hospital there after a severe beating from one of the *kapos*. The Russian soldiers who set all the surviving prisoners free handed out clothing and food, and separated those who were dying from those who might live. Mr Frank was given a bunk of his own in a different barracks. He immediately began asking people if they knew what had happened to his wife and daughters. He found out that his wife was dead. From that moment on, Mr Frank put all his efforts and hope into the belief that his daughters were still alive. Throughout his long journey by train and boat back to Amsterdam, he asked everyone he saw about Margot and Anne, but no one had any news.

Mr Frank arrived in Amsterdam on 3 June 1945. He went straight to Miep and Jan's apartment. His friends were overwhelmed to see him and told him that he could stay with them for as long as he wished. He explained that his wife was dead but that he was sure Margot and Anne were still alive.

Miep and Jan were also convinced that the two girls would return. Miep was so certain of this that she did not tell Mr Frank about the object she kept in her desk at work: Anne's diary. She had found it on the day of the arrest.

After the Gestapo had left the building, she, Jan and Bep had gone up to the annexe. Everything was a complete mess, with drawers pulled open and things scattered around. The floor was lost under heaps of books and papers. Looking closer, Miep realized that many of the papers belonged to Anne. She pointed out the diary to Bep, who picked it up. Quickly the two women sorted through the jumble for anything with Anne's handwriting on it. They also saved a photograph album, schoolbooks, reading books, Anne's shoe-bag embroidered with her initials, Anne's combing shawl and a little book of quotations she had compiled.

Returning to the office, Miep put the diary in her desk, determined to keep it under lock and key until she could hand it back to Anne. The diary was Anne's private property, Miep felt, and for this reason she said nothing to Mr Frank about it.

Immediately after his arrival in Amsterdam, Mr Frank went back to his old job at the Prinsengracht office. He was delighted to find Kugler and Kleiman there as well. Both had survived imprisonment in Dutch camps. While they had been in prison, Miep had taken charge of the business, but now everybody returned to their old jobs.

When Mr Frank wasn't at work, he spent every spare minute

questioning people, checking survivor lists, calling the Red Cross organization and placing adverts in the press, all in the hope of finding his daughters. In July he was visiting the Red Cross again when he saw a list with 'X's placed beside the names of those known to have died. Margot and Anne were listed – with crosses next to their names. The woman who had informed the Red Cross that the girls were dead was Janny Brilleslijper, who, together with her sister Lientje, had been among the last to see Anne and Margot in Belsen.

Mr Frank visited first Lientje and then Janny at their own homes shortly afterwards. Janny told him helplessly, 'Your daughters are . . . no more.' She watched in horror as he went white and fell into a chair, his last shred of hope gone.

When Miep heard the news, her first thoughts, apart from those of deep sorrow, were of Anne's diary; she knew that now she had to give it to Mr Frank. At this time he was sitting alone in his office, his head in his hands. She placed the small pile of papers and books on his desk and said softly, 'Here is your daughter Anne's legacy to you.' On top lay the red-and-white-checked diary. Miep left the room and Mr Frank opened the book in a daze. Its pages were untouched since Anne herself had last written on them. And there she was, on the first page, smiling up at him from a school photograph.

Slowly, Mr Frank began to read: 'Gorgeous photograph, isn't it!!! . . . On Friday, 12th June, I woke up at six o'clock and no wonder; it was my birthday . . .'

Although some survivors of the concentration camps made their way back home by ship and train, many remained in the Displaced Persons' Camps set up by the Allies. In December 1946, there were approximately 160,000 Jews living in West German Displaced Persons' Camps, the largest of which was in the old army camp in Bergen-Belsen. They were cared for by the British army and a number of international charities, who gave them food and other necessities.

There were many orphaned children in the Displaced Persons' Camps who needed special care after their experiences. Older children were given courses in various languages and took part in training programmes. Through the Youth Aliyah (Youth Immigration) organization, thousands of child survivors moved to Palestine, which became the Jewish State of Israel in 1948. Many felt that they could no longer live in the countries where they had been persecuted and had lost their families, and where anti-Semitism still existed. The creation of a safe Jewish homeland was very important to them for this reason.

Few of those children who had been sent to Britain in 1938 and 1939 on the *Kindertransports* were reunited with their families, almost all of whom had perished in the camps. Those who did find their parents again usually met each other as strangers. One young woman arranged for her mother to join her in England, but it was not as she had expected: 'It was a very strange experience. I was a little girl when I left and now I was a woman with a baby. Although it was August [my mother] was wearing a fur coat to bring it with her. She was a stranger to me;

it was terrible. It didn't get any easier; it was always difficult.'[129]

Approximately half the Jewish children who had hidden in Holland with foster families during the war were reunited with their parents. Others stayed with their host families, and some children were never told the truth about their backgrounds. Jewish children who had survived the camps were usually placed with foster families. Among them was Bronia Davidson, whose return to school left her feeling that 'death had taken its seat next to every child'. Not many of her schoolmates were as fortunate as Anna, a girl who had two parents still and a brother. For Bronia and her friends who had lost their parents, no one could ever hope to take their place or match the memory of their dead mothers.

Eva Geiringer, returning to Holland with her mother, found it very strange to move back into their former apartment. She recalls:

It felt so eerie to walk up the stairs. Inside it was as if the intervening years had not taken place. It was like stepping back in time – everything looked exactly the same. I wandered in and out of the rooms. Our furniture was in the same place, the curtains and the paintwork were unchanged and when I looked for the spot on my bedroom wall where Pappy [her father] had marked my height, it was still there. I went to the window and looked down into the square. Some children were playing at one end on the tarmac. Later I heard a taxi draw up in the street below and ran to open the door thinking, That's Pappy coming home with Heinz. But it was only a neighbour from across the hall.[130]

Eva's father and brother did not come back; both died in Mauthausen. Eva moved to London in the 1950s, where she married and had three children.

In the late summer of 1945, the first photographs of the concentration camps were published in newspapers around the world, shocking everyone. A year later, twenty-two leaders of the Nazi Party were put on trial before the Nuremberg Tribunal in Germany. Among them were Martin Bormann, who died before the execution date, and Hermann Goring, who killed himself rather than face the hangman's rope. Ten former Nazis were hanged on 16 October 1946, but many of those who had committed the most terrible crimes escaped justice, some by fleeing to Britain, the USA, Canada or Argentina, where they lived the rest of their lives without ever having to account for what they had done. One was Josef Mengele, Auschwitz's 'Angel of Death', who had been in charge of the selections and had performed medical experiments on hundreds of children. He escaped to Latin America and died in a swimming accident in Brazil in 1979.

In other countries, too, followers of the Nazi movement were put on trial. A few were hanged; most served only a few years in prison before being allowed to go free. Around 10,000 high-ranking Nazis managed to escape before the courts could catch up with them. Some were found by a concentration camp survivor, Simon Wiesenthal, who dedicated his life to hunting them down. Adolf Eichmann, who was largely in charge of the deportation process, was discovered living in Argentina by Israeli forces, who kidnapped him and brought him to trial in Israel. He was executed in 1961.

With the knowledge that both his children were dead, Mr Frank turned his efforts to finding people he had known before the war. He already knew that his friends who had hidden with him had died in different camps: Mr van Pels had been gassed in Auschwitz; Fritz Pfeffer had been transferred to Neuengamme concentration camp, where he died on 20 December 1944; Peter van Pels had been taken to Mauthausen on a death march and died on 5 May 1945; and Mrs van Pels died in an unknown location sometime before 8 May 1945. However, Anne's friends Lies Goslar and Jacqueline van Maarsen were still alive, and Mr Frank visited them often. He also wrote to his family in Switzerland, and in one letter he mentioned Anne's diary for the first time: 'I don't have any photos from the last years, of course, but Miep by chance saved an album and Anne's diary. But I didn't have the strength to read it all . . .'[131]

Soon, though, Mr Frank did begin to read the diary, and he found it difficult to put down. In his memoir, written many years later, he explained how he had felt at that time:

I began to read slowly, only a few pages each day, more would have been impossible, as I was overwhelmed by painful memories. For me, it was a revelation. There was revealed a completely different Anne to the child that I had lost. I had no idea of the depth of her thoughts and feelings . . . through Anne's accurate description of every event and every person, all the details of being in hiding become clear to me again.[132]

Mr Frank copied out the diary for his mother and sister in Switzerland, using a combination of Anne's original diary and the version she rewrote with a view to publication. He left out the parts he thought were less interesting and those entries in which Anne had written most angrily about her mother. He asked a friend to help him translate Anne's words from Dutch into German, because his mother knew no Dutch. Mr Frank mailed the whole thing, bit by bit, to Switzerland. His family there were astonished by it, as was his friend Werner Cahn, who told him he believed it should be published. Mr Frank thought about this and in the end decided that it was what Anne would have wanted. In his memoir he wrote, 'Anne would have so much loved to see something published . . . Initially I was very reluctant to publish, but then again and again I saw that my friends were right . . . the first edition of the diary appeared in 1947. Anne would have been so proud.'

The first Dutch edition, published in June 1947 on what would have been Anne's eighteenth birthday, sold out after six months, and a second edition was printed to meet demand. Mr Frank then sent the manuscript to publishers in Germany, who at first were undecided about bringing it out, feeling it might stir up a lot of emotion and guilt among the German people; but when it appeared in Germany in 1950, it sold well.

The diary was published in France and Japan that same year, where it was a success, and it appeared in Britain two years later. In America it became an instant bestseller.

By the mid 1950s, Mr Frank was spending several hours a day answering the letters he received from people who had read the diary. So popular had Anne's words become that in 1955 a play based on the diary opened in New York. It was highly successful and won many awards, going on tour throughout Europe. More than a million people saw the play in Germany, and sales of the diary soared. Youth groups there were established in Anne's name; schools and streets were named after her; a 2,000-strong crowd of teenagers travelled to Bergen-Belsen to commemorate her death; and at her former home in Frankfurt a plaque was attached to the wall. In 1957, a Hollywood film, *The Diary of Anne Frank*, was made.

Ever since the earliest publication of the diary, people had knocked on the door of 263 Prinsengracht, asking if they could look around the Secret Annexe. On 4 May 1960, it officially opened as a museum, called the Anne Frank House. Several changes were made to the front house where the offices and warehouse had been, but the annexe was kept as near as possible to how it had looked when Anne had been in hiding there. However, Mr Frank insisted that the annexe should remain empty; that was how it had been left after the arrest when the Nazis took away all their furniture and belongings.

After retiring from his businesses, Mr Frank moved to Switzerland. He had recently married again; Fritzi, his second wife, was the mother of Eva Geiringer and was herself a

Holocaust survivor. Fritzi helped her husband with the vast amount of correspondence produced by Anne's diary, which Mr Frank took with him to Switzerland. For the rest of his life, Mr Frank had to deal with extremists – people who said that his daughter's diary was a fake, written by someone else after the war to make money. The diary has undergone a series of scientific tests which have proved, beyond doubt, that it is a real document, written by Anne Frank. By no one else.

Mr Frank was in good health until the last year of his life, when he became ill with cancer. He died on 19 August 1980, at home in Switzerland. He was ninety-one years old. His second wife, Fritzi, outlived her husband by eighteen years. She spent the last months of her life living with her daughter in London.

Today, Miep Gies is the sole survivor of the five helpers. They were all given the highest honour possible to those who helped Jews during wartime: they were each awarded the accolade of 'the Righteous of the Nations' by Yad Vashem, the Holocaust Memorial Centre in Israel.

One thing has always intrigued readers of the diary over the years: who betrayed the occupants of the Secret Annexe to the Nazis? Two official investigations were held into the matter during Mr Frank's lifetime, but neither came up with a definitive answer. Until someone finds the receipt for the money the betrayer would have received for making that fateful telephone call (if the receipt still exists), the mystery, for many, will endure.

More than 20,000 Jewish communities were destroyed in Europe between 1940 and 1945. This figure, just like all the figures in the Holocaust, is so vast that it is hard to imagine what it actually represents.

Moniek Goldberg, who was a child survivor of the camps, was at first hurt by the people's failure to understand: 'But as I grew older I came to realize that I could not expect people to understand . . . The tragedy that befell our people was so great, so complete, that one cannot imagine it.'[133] Moniek emigrated from Britain to America and set up a successful business in Florida, where he lives with his family: 'When I look at my children and the children of my friends I realize more than ever that the victory is ours. We are able and useful citizens of society, with families who give us a lot to be proud of.'[134]

As many former concentration camps became museums, some survivors returned to the places where they had been imprisoned as children. For some, it gave them a feeling of strength. Erwin Baum returned to Auschwitz in June 1988 and walked around the barracks where he had slept, the bench where he had been beaten and the roll-call ground. When he left, it was because he wanted to and there on the other side of the gate was a taxi waiting to take him home. He remembers: 'I felt truly liberated for the first time.'

To those who say that the Holocaust didn't take place, and for those who still find it hard to understand what lies behind that figure of six million dead, Erwin has a firm answer: 'To the people who say there was no

Holocaust, tell them I was there. I'm real. It happened.'[135]

The Nazis who faced trial often claimed to have been merely acting on orders. But it *was* possible to resist those orders, which were to persecute and to kill. However evil their actions, the Nazis themselves were human beings, and many of them had homes and families they loved. Nevertheless, they chose to obey their orders. A few did resist, and some even rescued Jews. The case of Oskar Schindler is probably the best known, thanks to the book and then the film *Schindler's List*. He saved 1,200 Jews by giving them employment in his factories in Kracow and Brünnlitz between 1943 and 1944. At first, he seemed no different from any other Nazi: he lived in an apartment that had become empty when the Jewish family who owned it was turned out, and his factory had also belonged to a Jewish man. But gradually his eyes were opened to what was happening. He did all he could to protect the Jews who worked for him, even defying Nazi orders to move some of his employees to a slave labour camp; and when 300 of his female workers were sent to Auschwitz by mistake (during the transfer of his factory from one town to another), he personally visited the camp in order to get them out. His wife, Emilie, helped to care for many of the workers. When Schindler died in October 1974, more than 400 Jews whom he had rescued attended his funeral in Jerusalem, and today there are more than 6,000 descendants of 'Schindler Jews' living all over the world.

Many people claimed not to have known what was

happening to the Jews at the time. Some people simply did not want to know. If, instead of remaining silent, those people had spoken out, then the name 'Auschwitz' would have meant nothing today, and Anne Frank's diary, if it had existed at all, might have been no more than a young girl's private thoughts on growing up in the 1940s.

'Not to choose is also a choice,' wrote French philosopher Albert Camus. In the end, perhaps, it is the most dangerous choice of all. There are still cases of mass genocide taking place in the world today, but none of it is inevitable. It does not have to happen; it isn't fate. It is up to the individual, to all of us, to make a difference.

Anne's diary is now in Amsterdam once more, on display in the secret annexe. It has become a phenomenon, and Anne herself is now a historical figure. There are Anne Frank roses and tulips, statues, stamps, medals and awards, an Anne Frank Day, held annually on 12 June, and exhibitions about her throughout the world. A forest of 10,000 trees grows in her honour in Israel, a waxwork of her sits in Amsterdam's Madame Tussaud's, the Anne Frank House receives a million visitors each year – and yet, behind all this is a very ordinary girl . . . with an extraordinary gift for writing.

When, in her shuttered room, Anne mused, 'Will I ever be able to write anything great?'[136] she had no idea just how powerful her words would become. Her diary is now seen as 'the most important source of knowledge in the world today concerning the Holocaust'; 'the most widely read book of World

War II'; 'one of the key writings of the twentieth century';[137] and it is a set text in schools everywhere.

'I want to go on living, even after my death,' she wrote. Her diary has ensured that she will.

The Anne Frank Trust UK

The Anne Frank Trust UK, which was founded in 1991, is an educational charity and a sister organization of the Anne Frank House in Amsterdam.

Inspired by the spirit and vision of Anne Frank, the Trust's aim is to educate and motivate people to reject prejudice and injustice, and to build a society founded on mutual respect, responsibility and moral courage.

This aim is achieved through travelling exhibitions, educational programmes and civic events. With the Anne Frank Awards, the Trust also recognizes young people who have displayed moral courage and made a positive difference to those around them. If you would like to know more about the work of the Anne Frank Trust, wish to nominate someone for an Anne Frank Award, stage an Anne Frank exhibition or take part in any of our activities or educational programmes, please contact:

The Anne Frank Trust UK
Star House
104–108 Grafton Road
Kentish Town
London NW5 4BA
Phone: 020 7284 5858
Email: info@annefrankorg.uk
Website: www.annefrank.org.uk
Registered charity number: 1003279

Further Reading

Anne Frank

The Diary of Anne Frank: The Definitive Edition, Puffin
Books

For younger readers:
Anne Frank's Story, Carol Ann Lee, Puffin Books

For young adults:
Roses from the Earth: The Biography of Anne Frank,
Carol Ann Lee, Penguin Books

For all age groups:
Anne Frank: Beyond the Diary, Ruud van der Rol and
Rian Verhoeven, Puffin Books
The World of Anne Frank, Anne Frank Stichting,
Macmillan Books
A Friend Called Anne, Jacqueline van Maarsen and Carol
Ann Lee, Puffin Books
Memories of Anne Frank: Reflections of a Childhood

Friend, Alison Leslie Gold, Scholastic Press
Anne Frank Remembered, Miep Gies, with Alison Leslie Gold, Bantam Press

Other Diaries and Memoirs

For all age groups:
Eva's Story: A Survivor's Tale, Eva Schloss, with Evelyn Julia Kent, W. H. Allen
The Promise: The Moving Story of a Family in the Holocaust, Eva Schloss and Barbara Powers, Puffin Books

Acknowledgements

Carol Ann Lee gratefully acknowledges those authors and publishers who have granted permission to quote copyright material. While every effort has been made to trace all the copyright holders, the author apologizes for any oversights. Anyone believing they are entitled to exercise rights over these omissions is requested to contact the publisher.

The letters of the Frank family are used by the kind permission of Buddy Elias.

Extracts from *The Diary of Anne Frank: The Critical Edition* translated by Arnold J. Pomerans & B. M. Mooyaart-Doubleday. (Penguin Books, 1989). Copyright © Anne Frank-Fonds, Basle, Switzerland, 1986. English translation copyright © Doubleday, a division of Bantam Doubleday Dell Publishing Group Inc, and Penguin Books, Ltd, 1989. Reproduced by permission of Penguin Books Ltd.

Extract from *Anne Frank's Tales from the Secret Annexe* by Anne Frank, copyright © 1949, 1960 by Otto Frank.

Photo Credits

Sources

1. *Anne Frank's Diary*, 8 May 1944. All quotes from Anne's diary are taken from *The Diary of Anne Frank: Critical Edition* (Viking, 1989).
2. Anne Frank's baby book, archives of the Anne Frank-Fonds, Basel.
3. Ibid.
4. Anne's story was about Bad Paula during the First World War and how she accidentally found herself in a plane heading for the enemy territory of Russia. Eventually Paula found her way back to Germany, where she was happy to be with her family again. Because she wrote the story while she was in hiding from the Nazis, Anne felt compelled to add, 'We shouldn't forget that Paula was a German girl.'
5. Buddy Elias, author interview, Cheltenham, October 1997.
6. *Anne Frank: A History for Today*, written and published by the Anne Frank Stichting (Amsterdam, 1996), p. 20.
7. *A Tribute to Anne Frank*, by Anna G. Steenmeijer and Otto Frank (Doubleday, 1971), p. 13.
8. *Anne Frank: A History for Today*, exhibition panel.
9. Internet source.

10. *Anne Frank in the World*, by the Anne Frank House (Bert Bakker, 1985), p. 40.
11. *Anne Frank's Diary*, 15 June 1942.
12. *Anne aus Frankfurt*, exhibition panel.
13. Ibid.
14. Otto Frank, memoir, private collection of Buddy Elias.
15. *Stern* magazine, Anne Frank, letter, 21 May 1982.
16. *The Last Seven Months of Anne Frank*, by Willy Lindwer (Pantheon, 1991), pp. 16–17.
17. *A Tribute to Anne Frank*, p. 18.
18. Buddy Elias, author interview, Cheltenham, October 1997.
19. *Mail on Sunday*, *You* magazine, interview with Buddy Elias, 2 February 1997.
20. *Surviving the Fire*, by Lilo Klug, Internet source.
21. . . . *And the Policeman Smiled: 10,000 Children Escape from Nazi Europe*, by Barry Turner (Bloomsbury, 1990), p. 20.
22. *Anne Frank: A History for Today*, p. 68.
23. Buddy Elias, author interview, Cheltenham, October 1997.
24. . . . *And the Policeman Smiled*, pp. 28–9.
25. Ibid., p. 38.
26. *Anne Frank's Diary*, May 1939.
27. Ibid., Otto Frank, letter, May 1939.
28. Ibid., 28 September 1942.
29. *The War Against the Jews*, by Lucy S. Dawidowicz (Bantam Books, 1976), p. 143.
30. *Newsday* magazine, interview with Milly Stanfield, 16 March 1995.
31. Ibid.
32. *PRIVE* magazine, interview with Mrs Kuperus, 16 June 1979; Mrs Kuperus, in *The Footsteps of Anne Frank*, pp. 42–3.

33. Otto Frank, memoir, private collection of Buddy Elias.

34. *Autographs, Including Anne Frank Correspondence*, auction pamphlet from Swann Galleries, USA, Juanita Wagner, affidavit, 25 October 1988.

35. Ibid.

36. *New York Times*, interview with Betty Ann Wagner, 22 July 1988.

37. *The End of Innocence: Anne Frank and the Holocaust*, by Karen Shawn (Anti-Defamation League of B'nai B'rith, 1989), pp. 70–71.

38. *Anne Frank's Diary*, undated entry.

39. Ibid., 10 October 1942.

40. Jetteke Frijda, author interview, Amsterdam, March 1998.

41. Now Eva Schloss. She has written two books about her wartime experiences – see Further Reading.

42. Eva Schloss, author interview, London, January 1998.

43. *Anne Frank's Diary*, 6 January 1944.

44. Anne Frank, letter, June 1941, private collection of Buddy Elias.

45. Otto Frank, memoir, private collection of Buddy Elias.

46. *Sunday Oregonian*, interview with Laureen Nussbaum, 4 October 1992.

47. *A Friend Called Anne*, by Jacqueline van Maarsen and Carol Ann Lee (Puffin Books, 2004), p. 46.

48. *My Friend Anne Frank*, by Jacqueline van Maarsen (Vantage Press, 1996), pp. 21–2; and Jacqueline van Maarsen, author interview, Amsterdam, February 1998.

49. Ibid., pp. 46, 23.

50. Otto Frank, postcard, 14 September 1941, private collection of Buddy Elias.

51. Anne Frank, postcard, 14 September 1941, private collection of Buddy Elias.

52. *The War Against the Jews*, p. 169.

53. *Never Again: A History of the Holocaust,* by Martin Gilbert (HarperCollins, 2000), p. 70.

54. Since January 1992, the villa has been a museum and conference centre dedicated to the study of the Holocaust.

55. Quoted in *The Hidden Life of Otto Frank*, by Carol Ann Lee (William Morrow, 2002), p. 141.

56. Ibid.

57. *Anne Frank's Diary*, 20 June 1942.

58. Otto Frank, letter, 10 June 1971, private collection of Buddy Elias.

59. *Anne Frank's Diary*, 20 June 1942.

60. Jacqueline van Maarsen, author interview, London, January 1998.

61. *Tales from the Secret Annexe*, by Anne Frank (Penguin, 1982), p. 93.

62. Otto Frank, memoir, private collection of Buddy Elias.

63. Jacqueline van Maarsen, author interview, London, January 1998.

64. Ibid.

65. Anne Frank, letter, May 1942, private collection of Buddy Elias.

66. Margot Frank, letter, May 1942, private collection of Buddy Elias.

67. In 1946, work began on rebuilding the village, with money donated from all over the world. Survivors of that night still live in Lidice, where there is now a museum telling the story of 9 June 1942, and a rose garden and sculpture in memory of the lost children.

68. Eva Schloss, author interview, London, January 1998.

69. *Anne Frank and After: Dutch Holocaust Literature in*

Historical Perspective by Dick van Galen and Rolf Wolfswinkel (Amsterdam University Press, 1996), p. 48.

70. *Anne Frank's Diary*, 12 June 1942.

71. Jacqueline van Maarsen, author interview, London, January 1998.

72. *My Friend Anne Frank*, p. 54.

73. Ibid.

74. Edmond Silberberg, author interview, telephone, June 1998.

75. *Anne Frank's Diary*, 1 July 1942.

76. Otto Frank, postcard, 5 July 1942, private collection of Buddy Elias.

77. Anne Frank, postcard, 5 July 1942, private collection of Buddy Elias.

78. *My Friend Anne Frank*, pp. 27–8.

79. Now Ann Shore, and President of the Hidden Children Foundation.

80. Eva Schloss, author interview, London, January 1998.

81. *Eva's Story: A Survivor's Tale*, by Eva Schloss, with Evelyn Julia Kent (W. H. Allen, 1988), p. 44.

82. The van Rhijn family was reunited in May 1943 and lived together until the end of the war.

83. Internet source.

84. Ibid.

85. Ibid.

86. *Anne Frank's Diary*, 28 November 1942.

87. Ibid., 24 December 1943.

88. Ibid., 23 February 1944.

89. Ibid., 20 November 1942.

90. Ibid., 19 November 1942.

91. Ibid., 3 May 1944.

92. Ibid., 15 July 1944.

93. Footnote in *The Diary of Anne Frank: Critical Edition*, p. 273.

94. *Independent*, interview with Miep Gies, 4 May 1995.

95. *Anne Frank Magazine 1998*, interview with Miep Gies, pp. 26–8.

96. *Anne Frank's Diary*, 28 January 1944.

97. *The End of Innocence*, p. 75.

98. Translated from the Hungarian by Peter Hay. *Images of the Holocaust: A Literature Anthology*, edited by Jean E. Brown, Elaine C. Stephens and Janet E. Rubin (NTC Publishing 1996), p. 473.

99. *Anne Frank's Diary*, 3 February 1944.

100. Ibid., 25 March 1944.

101. Ibid., 1 August 1944.

102. Internet source.

103. Ibid.

104. *McCalls* magazine, interview with Otto Frank, January 1986.

105. *Anne Frank Remembered*, by Miep Gies, with Alison Leslie Gold (Bantam Press, 1987) p. 156.

106. Eva Schloss, author interview, London, January 1998.

107. Ibid.

108. *Anti-Defamation League Bulletin*, interview with Vera Cohn, June 1956.

109. *Ein Tagebuch für Anne Frank* film booklet, memoir by Lientje Brilleslijper (VEB Progress Film-Vertrieb, 1959).

110. Otto Frank, memoir, private collection of Buddy Elias.

111. Ibid.

112. *The Footsteps of Anne Frank*, by Ernst Schnabel, translated by Richard and Clara Winston (Longmans, Green & Co., 1959), p. 135.

113. *Ein Tagebuch für Anne Frank*, memoir by Lientje Brilleslijper.

114. Ibid.

115. *The Footsteps of Anne Frank*, p. 137.

116. *Ein Tagebuch für Anne Frank*, memoir by Lientje Brilleslijper.

117. Ibid.

118. Ibid.

119. Ibid.

120. Ibid.

121. Ibid.

122. Ibid.

123. Ibid.

124. Ibid.

125. Ibid.

126. *Eva's Story*, p. 147.

127. *Anne Frank and After*, p. 121.

128. *The Holocaust: The Jewish Tragedy*, by Martin Gilbert (Collins, 1986), p. 825.

129. . . . *And the Policeman Smiled*, p. 272.

130. *Eva's Story*, p. 216.

131. Otto Frank, letter, undated, private collection of Buddy Elias.

132. Otto Frank, memoir, private collection of Buddy Elias.

133. *The Boys: The Untold Story of 732 Young Concentration Camp Survivors*, by Martin Gilbert (Henry Holt & Co., 1997), p. 406.

134. Ibid., pp. 427–8.

135. *Images of the Holocaust*, pp. 522–3.

136. *Anne Frank's Diary*, 5 April 1944.

137. *War and Memory in the Twentieth Century*, by Martin Evans and Kenneth Lunn (Berg Publishers, 1997), pp. 3–16.